COURAGE

JOHN GILL

Courage
© 2023 by H&E Publishing

Series: John Gill on the spiritual life
Series Editor: Christopher Ellis Osterbrock

Published by: H&E Publishing,
West Lorne, Ontario, Canada
www.hesedandemet.com

All rights reserved. This book or any portion thereof may not be reproduced or used in any manner whatsoever without the express written permission of the publisher except for the use of brief quotations in a book review.

Source in Public Domain: John Gill, *A Body of Practical Divinity; or, a System of Practical Truths, Deduced from the Sacred Scriptures. Which (with the Two Former Volumes) Completes the Scheme of Doctrinal and Practical Divinity*, vol. 3 (London: George Keith, 1770), 40–51, 190–213.

Cover and layout design by Dustin Benge

Paperback ISBN: 978-1-77484-096-2
Ebook ISBN: 978-1-77484-097-9

THE John Gill PROJECT

In partnership with
The Andrew Fuller Center for Baptist Studies
& The London Lyceum

Editorial Board
Michael A. G. Haykin
Jonathan E. Swan
Christopher Osterbrock
Jordan L. Steffaniak
Garrett Walden
Chance Faulkner
David Rathel

John Gill on the spiritual life

Other books in the series:
What is theology?
Courage
Peace
Meekness
Humility
Joy

"All the divine perfections shine most illustriously in Christ, as he is the brightness of his Father's glory and the express image of his person."

JOHN GILL

CONTENTS

Series Preface		11
Introduction		13
The life and ministry of John Gill		
Courage *by John Gill*		31
1	Fortitude	33
2	Zeal	59
3	The Fear of God	85
4	Wisdom	125
Discussion questions		147
Scripture index		151

SERIES PREFACE

These six little volumes which make up the series John Gill on the spiritual life are designed with both the scholar and local church in mind. Each volume is transcribed from Gill's *A Body of Doctrinal and Practical Divinity* (1769–1770), and yet edited in such a way as to enable Gill's vocabulary, formatting (headings, subheadings, etc.), and syntax be read with ease by the 21st-century reader. Full names and dates of historical figures are also added at first use to bring greater clarity to the data. Included in each volume are discussion questions for the purpose of small groups or personal edification.

It is the endeavor of the John Gill Project to draw upon the rich spirituality at work in men like Gill, take it up fresh, and share it for the sake of godliness in our own churches today. May these sources be proven to magnify Christ and stir affections within his church.

Christopher Ellis Osterbrock
Series Editor

INTRODUCTION

The life and ministry of John Gill

"The Rev. Dr. John Gill was certainly one of the greatest and best of men."[1] Despite this superlative commendation, it is likely that you may have never heard of John Gill (1697–1771). Regrettably, Gill's name is unrecognizable among most Baptists. Historians certainly continue to discuss his life and thinking, but their numbers are small. As an historical figure, Gill remains in obscurity. This was not the case in his own day nor after his death, when his published writings were widely read and distributed in England and across the Atlantic to North America. One historian observes that "Gill was the natural theological leader of his

1   John Rippon, *A Brief Memoir of the Life and Writings of the Late Rev. John Gill, D. D.* (1838 repr. Harrisonburg, VA: Sprinkle Publications, 2006), 1.

day, for he had written more, published more, and defended more openly than any of his brethren ... He thus became the spokesman for Calvinist Dissent in general and for Baptists in particular."[2]

To rectify the lack of recognition of this towering figure in Baptist life, this modest biographical sketch seeks to introduce John Gill to new and inquiring audiences and thereby make him more well known. While Gill was an imperfect man, he is nevertheless worth remembering— and in several respects worth emulating. The facts of his life are by any standard extraordinary, Gill being a man of rare giftedness, industry, and constancy.

Childhood and education

John Gill was born on November 23, 1697, in Kettering, Northamptonshire. His parents Edward and Elizabeth raised him in a church of dissenters (non-Anglican Protestants in England). But in time they left to form a specifically Baptist congregation under the pastoral leadership of William Wallis (d. 1711), who had served as a teacher within

---

[2] Olin C. Robison, "Legacy of John Gill," *The Baptist Quarterly* 24, no. 3 (July 1971): 113.

their dissenting congregation.

Gill excelled in academics as a child, demonstrating unusual diligence and intellectual capability. By the age of twelve he had mastered Latin and attained proficiency in Greek that garnered him praise from pastors with whom he interacted at the local bookstore. The young Gill was so often at the local bookstore, devouring all the learning he could, that those who wanted to assert the surety of a fact would say that it is as sure "as John Gill is in the bookseller's shop."[3]

Despite Gill's prodigious learning as a child, his formal education abruptly concluded before the age of twelve when the local school master decided to take his students to the daily prayer services of the Church of England. Maintaining their fervent dissenting convictions, Gill's parents removed him from the school. And yet, despite numerous efforts to provide Gill with a formal education, he ended up working with his father part-time in the woolen trade until he was about nineteen years old.

Gill's removal from school did little to curb his

---

3 Rippon, *Memoir*, 4.

educational progress. He continued to master the classical curriculum by improving his facility in Greek and Latin and by studying logic, rhetoric, and philosophy. During this time Gill devoted himself to learning Hebrew and reading the Protestant scholastic authors, both of which became defining features of his writings. Gill's self-taught knowledge of Hebrew was a contributing factor to his reception of an honorary doctorate from Marischal College, Aberdeen University. Likewise, his study of the Protestant scholastic authors left an indelible mark on his approach to theology.

Conversion, ministry, and family

Around the age of twelve, Gill was converted while hearing William Wallis preach from Genesis 3:9. While Gill had previously experienced transient conviction of sin and fear of judgment, he had now come to experience his definite need of and reliance on Christ's righteousness. Shortly after this experience Wallis died and was succeeded in the pastorate by his son, Thomas Wallis (d.1726). It was Thomas Wallis who baptized Gill in a nearby river after Gill publicly professed his faith in Christ on November 1, 1716, at the age of nineteen.

Gill became a member of the church on the following Sunday, participated in the Lord's Supper, and, unexpectedly, preached his first sermon from Isaiah 53. This sermon, given during a prayer meeting, was received well and he was asked back the following week. Gill's second sermon at the prayer meeting was preached on 1 Corinthians 2:2.

The Kettering congregation very quickly discerned Gill's ministerial gifts, and with the recommendation of his friends, he soon moved to Higham Ferrers to assist pastor John Davis' newly-planted church. Gill had hoped that Davis would guide him in his studies, but that aspiration went unfulfilled. What may have seemed a disappointment soon turned into a blessing, since during his ministry in Higham Ferrers Gill met his wife-to-be, Elizabeth Negus.

John and Elizabeth were married in 1718 and stayed faithful in marriage until her death in October, 1764. By all available accounts they enjoyed an exemplary Christian marriage as both John and Elizabeth loved and served one another. While Elizabeth diligently worked to allow Gill fruitful hours of study and ministry, Gill served Elizabeth through years of "appalling health, caused by difficult pregnancies, miscarriages, still-births, and sickly infants."[4]

John and Elizabeth had numerous children together, although only three survived past infancy. And of these three, only two survived into adulthood. Their daughter Elizabeth died at the age of thirteen in 1738. In a demonstration of fortitude, Gill preached the sermon for both his deceased daughter and wife at their respective funeral services.

A call to London

It was not long after marrying Elizabeth that Gill returned to Kettering to assist his home church. His time back in Kettering, while short-lived, saw much fruitful ministry. Soon after arriving back in Kettering, Gill was invited to preach for a church at Horselydown in Southwark that had recently lost its pastor, Benjamin Stinton (1677–1719). Stinton was the son-in-law of the church's founder, Benjamin Keach (1640–1704), who had been influential

---

4   Sharon James, "'The Weaker Vessel': John Gill's Reflections on Women, Marriage and Divorce," in *The Life and Thought of John Gill (1697–1771): A Tercentennial Appreciation*, ed. Michael A. G. Haykin, Studies in the History of Christian Thought 77 (Leiden: Brill, 1997), 216.

amongst Particular Baptists. After his initial invitation, Gill came back to preach multiple times and it was determined that he should be considered to fill the pastoral vacancy.

A large majority of the church voted to elect Gill as pastor on November 13, 1719, but some opposed his election, including the church's deacons. Regardless of the opposition, Gill accepted the call to become their next pastor the following Sunday. Controversy erupted with the upshot that Gill's supporters separated from the other members while maintaining their identity as the congregation started by Keach. Gill was finally ordained as their pastor on March 20 of the following year.

Gill's conviction of his call to the church at Horselydown factored into his early success in London. As B.R. White wrote of Gill's tumultuous call to the church:

> For Gill's own stand was the key to the situation: if he remained firm long enough he could hope to live down the initial opposition; if he faltered, his own future as a minister in London was in grave doubt. Whilst there can be no doubt that his firmness stemmed from his own certainty that this was God's

will for him the prospect was one before which most men of his age would have quailed.[5]

His steadfastness in the face of opposition set the tone for his ministry and was a sign of things to come for Gill as a pastor-theologian.

Ministry in London
As Gill began his first full-time ministry, his preaching was met with great success. Early on the church found it difficult to accommodate all who wanted to hear the young preacher, even with their spacious accommodations.

Gill's preaching also led to his first publication in 1724, a funeral sermon for one of the church's deacons. It was also in this year that Gill began to preach sermons from the Song of Solomon that eventually became the basis for one of his most well-known works, *An Exposition of the Book of Solomon's Song*, published first in 1728. The book's republication in three editions during his life, as well as its posthumous republication, evince its popularity. Gill's memoirist

---

[5] B.R. White, "John Gill in London (1719–1729): A Biographical Fragment," *The Baptist Quarterly* 22 (1967–1968): 75.

notes that "the publication of this Exposition served very much to make Mr. Gill known."[6] The renowned preacher C.H. Spurgeon—who later pastored the same congregation in London—commented of this work that it was "The best thing Gill ever did ... Those who despise it have never read it, or are incapable of elevated spiritual feelings."[7]

Gill the controversialist

Early on Gill also established himself as a controversialist, or polemical writer. The first of such pieces centered on the doctrine of baptism. While Gill became conversant with the history of the church and drank especially deeply from the wells of the Reformed scholastic writers, he nevertheless maintained staunch Baptist convictions until his death. So when Gill penned one of his forays into controversial print in 1726, he wrote a defense of believer's baptism in response to Matthias Maurice (1684–1738), who pastored an Independent church in Northamptonshire. Gill's two

---

6 Rippon, *Memoir*, 24.
7 C H. Spurgeon, "Commenting and Commentaries: Two Lectures Addressed to the Students of The Pastor's College, Metropolitan Tabernacle, Together with A Catalogue of Biblical Commentaries and Expositions," in *Lectures to My Students: Four Volumes in One* (Pasadena: Pilgrim Publications, 1990), 113.

works written in response to Maurice furthered his reputation, not only among Baptists in England, but also in North America.

Many, if not most, of Gill's writings were occasioned by the spread of some doctrine or idea he believed was injurious to the gospel. Gill published his *Exposition of the Book of Solomon's Song* at the behest of his church, but Gill's main aim in publishing it was to defend the book's authority and canonicity in light of recent challenges. The same year, Gill published *The Prophecies of the Old Testament, Respecting the Messiah, Considered and Proved to Be Literally Fulfilled in Jesus* to demonstrate the fulfillment of messianic prophecies in Jesus through a literal interpretation of Scripture.

Gill willingly engaged in controversy for the sake of what he believed was true, even at the risk of personal cost. In a debate with Abraham Taylor (fl. 1726–1740) over the doctrine of justification, he was cautioned against furthering their disagreement. He was told that continued debate could result in a loss of reputation and income if he lost the support of some wealthy subscribers to his books. Nevertheless, Gill is reported to have responded, "Don't tell me of losing … I value nothing, in comparison of Gospel truths. I am not afraid to be poor."⁸

Gill not only resisted careerist tendencies, but he unrelentingly prosecuted his arguments. John Wesley, with whom Gill controverted, said that "he is a positive man, and fights for his own opinions through thick and thin." Augustus Toplady (1740–1778) held Gill's argumentative efforts in high regard when he wrote the following complimentary comparison: "I believe it may be said of my learned friend, as it was of the Duke of Marlborough, that he never fought a battle which he did not win."⁹

Gill the pastor-theologian

Within a decade of starting his ministry in London, Gill had earned sufficient recognition to warrant an invitation to establish a weekly lecture series organized by a group of men from multiple denominations. Starting in 1729, Gill dedicated himself to these Wednesday evenings for over twenty-six years. During this time, Gill adapted many of his lectures into print, including his *The Doctrine of The Trinity*, *The Cause of God and Truth*, and his *Exposition of the Old*

---

8   Rippon, *Memoir*, 37.
9   Rippon, *Memoir*, 65.

and New Testament. He finally resigned the lecture in 1756 in order to preserve his energy for the completion of his *Exposition of the Old Testament*.

Throughout the seventeenth century, the doctrine of the Trinity became a controversial doctrine and its denial led many away from the orthodox Christian faith. Gill, sensitive to the influence of these errors early in his ministry, used his Wednesday evening lectures to write *The Doctrine of the Trinity*, published in 1731. In this book, Gill sought to biblically prove the doctrine of the Trinity, setting down God's unity of essence and plurality of persons—Father, Son, and Spirit. The importance of defending this doctrine continued during Gill's ministry, evidenced by the book's republication in 1752. The issue of Trinitarian doctrine arose as an issue within Gill's church as they were required to disfellowship members who denied Christ's eternal Sonship. As a response, Gill proposed, and the church agreed, to add language to their statement of faith in order to more clearly define their Trinitarian convictions. And in the composition of his massive *Body of Doctrinal and Practical Divinity*, written in the very late stages of his life, Gill added substantial chapters to describe how each of the persons of the Trinity is distinguished from each other in the divine nature. Gill considered the Trinity a central doctrine that affects both one's belief and Christian experience.

Another of Gill's writings that emerged from the Great Eastcheap lectures and that defined his thinking was *The Cause of God and Truth*. Written and released in four parts between 1735–1738, Gill sought to respond to Daniel Whitby's *Discourse on the Five Points*. For Gill's part, he wrote to establish the theological and rational basis of Calvinism, as well as prove that church history did not favor the Arminian position. Even those who know little about Gill know something of his Calvinism. As Nettles has aptly written, "Seeking to convince people familiar with Baptist history that Gill fits within the frame of Calvinistic theology would be like trying to convince a veterinarian that cows give milk. 'Gill is a Calvinist' is a virtual redundancy."[10] Gill's belief in God's sovereign choice in election and salvation as a free gift of grace formed definitive features of his theological outlook.

---

10   Thomas J. Nettles, By His Grace and For His Glory: A Historical, *Theological and Practical Study of the Doctrines of Grace in Baptist Life* (Cape Coral, FL: Founders Press, 2006), 23.

INTRODUCTION

As a pastor, Gill considered it his duty to feed his flock with God's word. Week in and week out for fifty-one years Gill went before his congregation and exposited God's word. The fruit of Gill's intense study, diligent preparation, and constant preaching of God's word became a massive and priceless gift to the church—a commentary on the entire Bible.

Each year, from 1746–1748, Gill published a successive volume of his *Exposition of the New Testament*. In recognition of Gill's accomplishment, Marischal College at Aberdeen University awarded Gill with a Doctorate of Divinity. Nearly a decade later in 1757 and 1758, Gill published an *Exposition of the Prophets* in two volumes, works which "gave him unfading honours, and induced such who have made those parts of the divine writings their study, to say, that if the words of Dr. Gill pre-eminently embrace almost every branch of sacred theology, *prophecy is his forte.*"[11]

To complete his herculean *Exposition* of the whole Bible, Gill published the remainder of his Old Testament commentary in four volumes, each volume appearing in

---

11   Rippon, *Memoir*, 74.

successive years from 1763–1766. In total, his *Exposition* of both the Old and New Testament numbered nine volumes.

With a firm grasp of ancient history and the original languages, Gill's exposition is marked by historical and linguistic sensitivity. His expertise in rabbinical literature conspicuously appears throughout, but his exegetical writings are defined chiefly by his theological exegesis guided by the analogy of faith.

Near the end of his life, Gill spent more than five years preaching the substance of what would become his *Body of Doctrinal Divinity*. He published this two-volume work of systematic theology in 1769 and followed the next year with his *Body of Practical Divinity*, which he also composed of Sunday sermons. The creation of this *Body of Doctrinal and Practical Divinity* serves as the definitive statement of Gill's doctrine, and can be considered the fruit of his decades of exegesis and a symbol of his continuity with the Protestant scholastic tradition.

As Gill's physical abilities waned in his old age, his church suggested they hire a co-pastor. Gill replied with a letter of resignation, questioning the biblical warrant for co-pastors. Distressed by Gill's response, the church pleaded with him to remain as pastor, expressing that it was their "fixed desire, and Continual Prayer, that you may live and die in that endear'd Relation."[12] Gill remained their pastor until his death on October 14, 1771, having held that office more than fifty-one years.

Gill's significance today

From an historical perspective, Gill's legacy has received mixed reviews. While there are some who have cast him as the principal reason for Particular Baptist decline, others have lauded him as a defender of the faith who helped preserve the gospel amidst a decaying spiritual culture. Regardless of any negative effects related to his alleged hyper-Calvinism, Gill stood firmly against the winds of culture that so fiercely ravaged other denominations. In the face of Enlightenment rationalism, deism, and Unitarianism, Gill held firm to the inerrancy and authority of the Scriptures and defended the biblical doctrine of the Trinity. Gill's insistent confessionalism served as a stabilizing example during a time that Gill himself called "a day of darkness

---

12 George M. Ella, *John Gill and the Cause of God and Truth* (Durham: Go Publications, 1995), 240–242.

and gloominess." Regardless of where his culture stood, Gill stood on the unshakable foundation of Scripture.

In these and other respects, Gill stands as a spiritual example to follow. Whether one considers his life as a husband, father, or pastor, Gill exemplified a life of faithfulness and unshakable trust in Christ. Suffering the loss of numerous children in infancy, his daughter Elizabeth as a child, or his wife in old age, Gill fixed his heart firmly on the hope he held in Christ.

When Gill died he left behind the fruit of his faithful ministry in writing. In an estimated total of 10,000 pages, Christians today may still be taught by this Baptist luminary on a wide variety of topics ranging from linguistics to historical theology.

Gill's indefatigable study serves as an example to all Christians, but especially ministers. Gill so prized theological education he went to incredible lengths to teach himself Hebrew as well as other subjects. Gill never regretted these efforts that enriched his ministry and writings. So, too, will all Christians benefit from diligent study of God's word.

Jonathan E. Swan

COURAGE

JOHN GILL

ONE

Fortitude

Saints are to be humble, self-denying, submissive to the will of God, and patient towards all men in all things. However, they are not to indulge in spinelessness or a meanness of spirit. Christians are to show firmness of mind, resolution, undaunted courage, fortitude of soul, and a manly spirit, which is not at all unbecoming the Christian. "For God has not given us the spirit of fear, but of power, of love, and of a sound mind," and so the Christian should play the man, act the manly part, show themselves to be men.[1] As much as the Christian pursues wisdom, so should he pursue courage. When Paul writes, "Be watchful, stand firm in the faith, act

---

1   2 Timothy 1:7.

like men, be strong," this is not merely strength of body, but fortitude of mind.[2] This fortitude is the subject now to be treated in the following chapter.

The nature of Christian fortitude

It is not a natural fortitude which is meant throughout Scripture, for natural fortitude may be in beasts as well as in men. This kind is found in the lion, "which is the strongest among beasts, and turns not away from any,"[3] and its courage is equal to its strength. But such natural animosity, or greatness of mind, found among men is not properly virtue, much less grace, as is Christian fortitude.

Christian fortitude does not lie in bold and daring enterprises, as when a man attempts things arduous and difficult, and encounters dangers. When performing difficult tasks for his own sake the daring man may rush into them unnecessarily and unwarily, without any consultation and deliberation, and without having any good end in view to be answered. This practice is no other than audaciousness, likewise, considered temerity or rashness—this is not true

---

2 1 Corinthians 16:13.
3 Proverbs 30:30.

fortitude.

True Christian fortitude is also to be distinguished from civil fortitude, or what is exercised in war, in a military way. Though civil fortitude may bear some resemblance to the Christian, the two are distinguished from each other. Often it is the case that civil fortitude is just a false appearance. Men will make a show of courage through fear of disgrace, rebukes from superiors, military discipline, or of being taken prisoner and becoming captive. Such a fortitude may also arise from natural confidence in bodily strength, in the strength and safety of armor, in military skill, and through ignorance of the strength of the enemy. Great civil strength is found usually through the hope of honour and the applause of men, and sometimes of the spoil. At most and best, civil fortitude is exercised for a person's own good and the good of their country, which is commendable.

Yet, Christian fortitude is concerned about things which are made apparent as to the will of God and therefore exercised in obedience to his will. The strength of fortitude is found for the sake of a saint doing his duty, and with a pure view to the honour and glory of God. Christian fortitude is observed in the saint's trusting in and depending upon

God's power, strength, and grace to carry the saint through whatever he is called to do or suffer in the performance of God's will. For the sake of God's glory, the saint is not deterred by any difficulties that occur, or dangers to which he may be exposed—this is fortitude becoming a Christian.

The necessity of Christian fortitude
When we consider the many duties of religion to be performed by us, it requires great boldness of faith, and confidence in Christ for grace and strength. We are to be steadfast and immoveable, with constancy and perseverance, both in public and private life, as well as in our relative, social, and personal spheres. When our own weakness is considered—that without Christ we can do nothing—then Christ is strengthening his saints through fortitude in all these things.

Since the Christian has so many difficulties and dangers to encounter, so many discouragements in the way, so many trials, temptations, tribulations, and afflictions from various quarters, he must be a man of fortitude not to be moved by these things. He must bear all these dangers and difficulties with an invincible courage and constancy. Even more difficulties may be added regarding the numerous enemies with whom he must grapple—enemies mightier than he, who are lively and strong. Some are not flesh and blood as he is, but above his match. The Christian must battle principalities and powers, and spiritual wickednesses in high places.

Good saints dwell in a sinful world, so called "this present evil world,"[4] and are to live soberly, righteously, and godly in it. The Christian is to bear the vexation arising from the filthy conversation of the wicked—as was the case of Lot—and to bear a testimony against them. Saints are to endure suffering from the wicked, by their mockery, insults, and injuries, who are for war when they are for peace. And to heed this Christian calling requires great fortitude of mind, as their souls are sometimes among lions, at least men comparable to such beasts, just as David's soul was.[5] Therefore, the saints have need to be just as "bold as lions,"[6] as the righteous man is.

Now this being the case, and these the circumstances

---

[4] Galatians 4:1.
[5] Psalm 7:2; 35:17; 57:4.
[6] Proverbs 28:1.

of the Christian, he has need of great fortitude of mind, strength, and grace from above to support him. He has need to be "strong in the Lord, and in the grace that is in Christ Jesus."[7] He has need to be fortified with the love of God, with the promises of the gospel, and with fresh supplies of grace and strength from Christ. These are the type of things that will more largely appear in the following discourse.

How fortitude is demonstrated

Now we come to consider what this fortitude consists of in the Christian mind, and how it shows itself in the diligent believer.

The performance of religious exercises

Fortitude is first shown through family worship, which undoubtedly is incumbent on the people of God. A man is to distinguish himself among his neighbors like Joshua did: "As for me, and my house, we will serve the Lord,"[8] so let others do what they will—this shows religious fortitude of mind. As an example of this, consider when a man first sets

---

7   2 Timothy 2:1.
8   Joshua 24:15.

up family prayer in his house. Suppose the master of a family is the only one in it called by grace; if he has an irreligious spouse, irreligious children and servants, he should still see it his duty to call them together once a day to pray with them. For this man to fall to his knees alongside his wife, children, and servants, even while they sneer and laugh at him (even secretly), this requires a fortitude of mind. If this is not the case, or he lives alone, then his fortitude may be shown among wicked neighbors. Were a Christian to pray, to read the Scriptures, or sing the praises of God, with or without some Christians in his family—and to do so even while exposed to the ridicule and contempt of his neighbors and community—this is an instance and evidence of fortitude.

Submission to Christ's lordship
Fortitude is exhibited in a man's giving up himself to a church of Christ, to walk with it in all the commandments and ordinances of the Lord. For a man to attend public worship on Lord's days is no great trial of his fortitude because it is what his neighbors also do. However, let this man separate himself from the world and stand out from among

them—is he then able to demonstrate his resolve to worship? If a man will give himself up to the Lord in a public manner, and to his people in a church state, truly this will try and show his fortitude. To demonstrate this submission in such a public way is practically saying, "I am not of the world, and belong to another;" this will unavoidably draw the hatred of the world upon him. He will be liable to be challenged in a reproachful way, "You are also one of them," as Peter was by a man in the high priest's hall, and who did not have courage enough to own it but denied it.

Obedience to believer's baptism
Christian fortitude is shown in submitting to the ordinance of baptism as it was first delivered and practiced. This fortitude is demonstrated when a man argues against the sprinkling of infants, as it is an innovation, and openly avows the true doctrine of baptism as administered only to those who profess faith in Christ by immersion. If he will proceed to follow Christ in this now despised ordinance, he must be content to be nicknamed, to have reproach plentifully poured upon him not only by the profane world, but by the generality of the professors of religion. When a man is

satisfied that what he is called to do is his duty commanded by God, then he will take courage and "be strong, and do it." This is just as David advised his son Solomon with respect to building the temple. And so this duty ought to be obeyed, though attended with some things disagreeable to flesh and blood. We are encouraged in fortitude as with the divine presence, as Zerubbabel, Joshua, and the Jews were to "be strong ... and work; for I am with you, says the Lord of hosts."[9]

The apostles demonstrated this fortitude when ordered by Christ to preach his gospel, administer his ordinances, and teach men to observe all that he commanded—to which he encouraged them: "Behold, I am with you always, to the end of the age!"[10] These types of references will inspire a good man with courage to do his duty and give resolve when otherwise he would be deterred by the edicts or severe menacing of men.

We see this resolve displayed in the three companions of Daniel who bravely refused to worship Nebuchadnezzar's image, though threatened to be cast into a fiery furnace, and

9 Haggai 2:4.
10 Matthew 28:20.

so they were. When Daniel was under an edict obtained from the king that no man should pray to his God for such a time under the penalty of being cast into the den of lions, he boldly went on in the performance of his duty. He even opened his windows, and prayed to the God of heaven, as he had in times past.

The apostles held fast to duty when, strictly charged by the rulers to preach no more in the name of Jesus and were severely threatened if they did, with great firmness of mind and intrepidity answered, "We ought to obey God rather than man."[11] Promises of grace and strength will animate saints to a cheerful obedience to the will of God, and to the discharge of their duty amidst all discouragements and difficulties. God says, "as their day is, their strength will be;"[12] that is, his strength will be made perfect in their weakness, his grace be sufficient for them. He bids them, "Fear not, I am with thee; I will strengthen thee!"[13] This will give them a fortitude of mind which will overcome all their fears; and they will say with David: "The Lord is my light and my

11 Acts 5:29.
12 Deuteronomy 33:25.
13 Isaiah 41:10.

salvation, whom shall I fear? The Lord is the strength of my life, of whom shall I be afraid?"[14] Active fortitude is that which shows itself in doing the duties of religion.

In bearing afflictions with constancy

Fortitude is revealed in the Christian enduring sufferings with a firmness of mind, whether these afflictions are from the hands of God or men. This constancy and endurance may be called passive fortitude.

Concerning afflictions from the hands of God, we read most notably of Job who was sensible he received his afflictions, his loss of substance, children, and health all from God's providential hand; so, he bore it all with an invincible fortitude of mind. This fortitude appears when a man's spirit does not sink under the weight of an affliction, but has strength of mind and a fortitude of soul under adversity. Scripture shares that "the spirit of a man," of a saint animated with Christian courage, "will sustain his infirmity," his bodily infirmity, wearisome diseases or racking pains, sustained by the graces of Christian fortitude. Such a saint will

---

14 Psalm 27:1, 3, 4.

go through any severe operation he may be called to, with a becoming resolution and manliness.[15]

Where fortitude will sustain Christians through the afflictions brought on by the hands of men, we understand this to be when saints are called to suffer shame and reproach for the sake of Christ. This is observed best when hardships arise especially for the sake of the gospel, the truths and ordinances of it. Saints, in imitation of Christ and even his fortitude, despise the shame of reproach, and account it an honour to bear it for his sake.

Saints are called in their suffering as Christians, to not be ashamed, but rather glorify God, acknowledging the Spirit of glory and of God resting upon them. When they endure cruel mockings, as some of the Old Testament saints did, the saints of Christ bear them patiently, and with an invincible firmness of mind—as Christ did on the cross.

We see how the apostles bore these afflictions from the hands of men, when made a spectacle to the world, to angels, and men. They were made the filth of the world, and the offscouring of all things, reviled, persecuted, and defamed.

---

15   Proverbs 18:14; 24:10.

These former saints bore all with a temper of mind which showed them to be possessed of Christian fortitude.

Others have suffered confiscation of their belongings, and took joyfully "the spoiling of their goods,"[16] as the believing Hebrews did, and as our forefathers in the last century did when they were under persecution. Others, in joining with the apostles of Christ and Old Testament saints, suffered "scourging, bonds, and imprisonment."[17] We witness particularly the apostle Paul, who received from the Jews on five occasions the scourging of forty stripes save one, and was beaten three times with rods which perhaps left those marks on him which he calls, "the marks of the Lord Jesus" he bore "in his body,"[18] and he was in prisons frequently. Paul seems to take pleasure, and even to glory, in being a prisoner of Christ, in chains for his sake. Such a heroic spirit, and with such fortitude was he endued, that none of these things moved him from the gospel of the grace of God.

Death itself, in its most formidable shapes, has been endured by the saints with an invincible courage. This is

16 Hebrews 10:34.
17 Hebrews 11:36.
18 Galatians 6:17.

clearly observed in the martyrs through the ten pagan persecutions, and by the witnesses of Jesus against the papal hierarchy. We see the courage of facing death particularly by our own reformers in the days of queen Mary I of England (1516–1558), such as Hugh Latimer (1487–1555), Nicholas Ridley (1500–1555), John Bradford (1510–1555), and others. These heroes were surrounded with kindling, and while the flames surrounded them, they expressed their undaunted courage, firmness, and fortitude of mind to the last. These, with multitudes of others, loved not their lives to death.

Christian fortitude and spiritual warfare

There is a warfare for men on earth, and especially for good men—the good soldiers of Christ who must endure hardness to which Christian fortitude is necessary. Therefore, saints should be, as Joshua was exhorted to be, "strong and courageous,"[19] when he was called to fight the Lord's battles, and against the enemies of the people of Israel. The same sentiment comes to us as when Joab said to Abishai his

---

19   Joshua 1:9.

brother, "Be of good courage, and let us be courageous for our people, and for the cities of our God."[20]

Defending the cause of truth

Christian fortitude is needed in the defense of the cause of God and truth on the behalf of the church of God. Solomon's bed, which is symbolically understood as the church of Christ, is said to have "sixty valiant men around it, the valiant of Israel,"[21] and these men are valiant for the truth on earth. Such men are concerned for the welfare of the church, and for the protection of it from errors and heresies, and they will not give way—not for a single hour—that the truth of the gospel may continue with the church, and its ordinances remain pure and incorrupt. And these are not only the ministers of the word who are called to defend the gospel, and who war a good warfare, who fight the good fight of faith, who speak with the enemy in the gate, and who are bold in their God to preach the gospel of Christ as it ought to be spoken. No, not only ministers, but all who profess Christian faith, and all who are members of the church of

---

20 2 Samuel 10:12.
21 Song of Solomon 3:7.

Christ. All the saints should "stand fast in one Spirit, striving together for the faith of the gospel," and should contend earnestly, even to an agony, "for the faith once delivered to the saints," and in so doing they show a fortitude of mind.[22]

Fighting sin and temptation

This fortitude also appears in fighting against spiritual enemies such as sin, and the lusts of it, which war against the soul. The law in the flesh is warring against the law of the mind, the flesh lusting against the spirit, so the mind and the body are a company of two armies. Now one with Christian fortitude will strive against sin, be an antagonist to it, and act the manly part against it. He will wrestle against Satan, his principalities and powers, and give no place to the devil. The Christian will resist him by faith; and Satan, when resisted, will flee for he is an errant coward and does not care to be handled with the armor of Christians. Those young men who are strong, possessed of Christian fortitude, and in whom the word of God dwells, overcome the wicked one. The world, with all its flattering lusts and frowning fury, is

---

22   Philippians 1:28; Jude 1:3.

overcome by the saints in their exercise of faith.[23]

Persevering in the battle

The saints have great reason to be of good courage, even while the church is currently under attack. There are more for them, than they that are against them. Truly if God is for the saints—and he is—then who can be against them? Through God, his church will do valiantly. The Christian is engaged in a good cause; he wars a good warfare and fights the good fight of faith. He has a good captain under whose banner he fights—the great captain of salvation. Saints are equipped with good weapons: the shield of faith, the helmet of salvation, and the sword of the Spirit. These God-given weapons are not carnal but spiritual and mighty, and are those that are meant to be proved, and with confidence made use of. These spiritual weapons are sure of victory even before the battle. For all their enemies are conquered, sin is made an end of, Satan and his power of death is destroyed, the world is overcome by Christ, the warfare is accomplished, and believers are made more than conquerors

---

23 1 John 5:4–5.

through him that has loved them. Therefore, saints may be sure of the crown of life, of the righteousness and glory laid up for all that love the appearing of Christ. This promise of perseverance should serve to fill them with an holy fortitude in their spiritual warfare.

Christian fortitude in the hour of death

Death is very terrible to nature, and to natural men; Aristotle even calls it "the most terrible of all terribles." No wonder he should call it so, since he adds, according to his opinion, it is "the end of all things, and that to one that is dead there is neither good nor evil."[24] Such a notion of death as being an extinction is indeed terrible! This wise man in Ecclesiastes suggests what is most grieving, distressing, and intolerable. He uses the phrase, "more bitter than death," as if there was nothing more grievous than it.[25] To Christless sinners, death is the "king of terrors," and even some gracious persons have been subject to the bondage of fear of death throughout their lifetime. As formidable as death is, there are some things which fortify the Christian against

---

24 Aristotle, *The Nicomachean Ethics*, III.6.
25 Ecclesiastes 7:26.

the fear of it.

Death is no longer a punishment

Christ has abolished death as a penal evil, so that it will never be inflicted on the believer by way of punishment. The sting of death is sin, and a very venomous sting it is, yet it is taken away by Christ. Death thus armed with sin is to be feared, but when its sting is taken out of it by Christ, it is no longer to be dreaded. We are naturally afraid of any insect with a sting, but if its sting is removed we have no fear of it, though it flies and buzzes about us. So, in a view of death being unstung, the believer may sing and say, "Death, where is thy sting?"[26] and be fearless of it.

Death is a privilege

Death is a privilege and blessing to believers. Death has a place in the saints' inventory of goods that belong to them: "death is yours." It is a means of happiness to them, "Blessed are the dead that die in the Lord,"[27] since they are delivered through death from all evils, from all outward afflictions

26 1 Corinthians 15:55.
27 Revelation 14:13.

and inward troubles.

By death, the saints are delivered from a body of sin and death, under which they now groan as being burdened, but in death they are delivered from the world and its snares, and from Satan and his temptations. Therefore, the dead in Christ are happier than living saints because they are with Christ, enjoying communion with him and beholding his glory, which is much better than to be in the present state.

Raised from death

Death, though it separates soul and body, and one friend from another, it does not separate from the love of God, but leads believers to the more glorious discoveries and enjoyment of God's love. It is precious in the sight of the Lord, and therefore saints should not shrink at it themselves.

Death is but once, as "it is appointed for man to die once,"[28] and no more. Death will soon be over, and usher in our happy endless eternity. When the body dies the soul does not, but immediately enters a state of glory. Death is the inlet into and the beginning of that eternity—the birthday of

---

28   Hebrews 9:27.

an eternal world of bliss. Following this entrance into glory there will be a resurrection of the body, when it will be fashioned like to the glorious body of Christ, raised in power, in glory, and as fits a spiritual body. The saints are not losers but gainers by death, and therefore do not need to fear it. The resurrection of the body yields comfort in the view of death, as well as a view to present afflictions, as it did to Job.[29]

Death defeated finally

Even though it may be viewed as gain to the saints, death is an enemy as it is contrary to nature. It is the last enemy that will be destroyed; and when death is conquered, the victory will be complete over every enemy, sin, Satan, the world, and the grave. Besides these things which may serve to promote a fortitude of mind against the fear of death, it may be proper frequently to meditate upon death and to think of it as near at hand. There is real benefit to making death familiar to us, by saying as Job did, that corruption is our father now,[30] but considering death will lead us to our

29 Job 19:25–27.
30 Job 17:14.

God and true Father, to our home, to our Father's house. By going to bed and resting in death we sleep well there in the arms of Jesus.

God gifts fortitude

Fortitude is not from our own nature but it is a grace gift from God. He is the one that gives strength and power to his people, and not bodily strength only but spiritual strength. He is the one that girds his people with strength, with holy fortitude, fills them with spiritual courage, strengthens their hearts, and fortifies them against their spiritual enemies.

The cause of fortitude

The efficient cause of Christian fortitude is God—the Father, the Son, and the Spirit. God the Father is prayed to for it, and he is the one who establishes the saints in Christ, gives them stability and firmness of mind.[31]

God the Son, who is Christ, calls the saints to "be of good cheer," to be strong and of good courage in the midst of tribulation. He calls them to this strength since he has

---

31   Ephesians 3:14, 16; Colossians 1:11–12.

overcome the world. It is "through him" who "strengthens" them that the saints can do and suffer all things for his sake.

God the Spirit, the Spirit of the Lord, rests as a "Spirit of counsel and might" on Christ the head. Those who are members of the body of Christ likewise have the Spirit of the Lord resting upon them. This counsel and might is a grant of God, a free grace gift of his, that his people be "strengthened with power through his Spirit in their inner being."[32]

The means of fortitude

The word of God is the means of producing and increasing Christian fortitude. God's word is not only a part of the spiritual armor, called the "sword of the Spirit," but has its place and abiding in the heart. Through the word of God in the heart of the saint, the Christian is fortified against spiritual enemies and victory is gained over them.[33] The precious promises contained in God's word serve greatly to animate the saints, and to inspire them with fortitude amidst all surrounding evils.

---

32   Isaiah 11:2; Ephesians 3:16.
33   1 John 2:14; Revelation 12:11.

Such a temper and disposition of mind is attainable by faith, prayer, and waiting upon God. By faith men so eminent for their fortitude of mind performed those heroic exploits we read of in Hebrews 11:1–40. These are those heroes who by faith subdued kingdoms, stopped mouths of lions, quenched the violence of fire, endured with such greatness of mind the many evils they did, and through constant prayer these saints obtained a spirit of boldness both with God and before men. By waiting upon the Lord in religious exercises spiritual strength or fortitude is renewed, hence the exhortation, "Wait on the Lord."[34]

Other means

The patterns of courage, the examples of fortitude in the saints who have gone before us, will lead us to find the grace of strength. The prophets, apostles, first Christians, and martyrs in all ages are a means for promoting a like disposition, particularly that cloud of heroes just mentioned. We should place, above all, Christ himself as the pattern of courage set before us, whom we are directed to look to and consider, "so

---

34   Psalm 27:14.

that we may not grow weary and fainthearted."[35]

And so, the love of God and the senses of that love carry us forward in fortitude through a persuasion of interest in God's love. Fortitude is grown in acknowledging that nothing shall separate us from the love of God, in acknowledging that his perfect love casts out fear, and discovering that such love inspires with fortitude against every enemy.[36]

---

35 Hebrews 12:1–3.
36 Romans 8:35, 38, 39; 1 John 4:18.

TWO

Zeal

Zeal is an ardour of mind, a fervent affection for some person or thing; this includes an indignation against everything supposed to be pernicious and hurtful to the object of zeal. Christian zeal is a divine grace that is evidenced through vehement affection for God and his glory. This affection produces an earnest study by all proper means to promote his glory and with a resentment of everything that tends to obscure or hinder it.

Christian zeal is hot, burning, flaming love, which cannot be quenched by water, drowned by floods, abated, restrained, or stopped by any difficulties in the way.[1] The term

---

1   Song of Solomon 8:6–7.

is sometimes used for that strong affection God bears to his people, expressed by his earnest care of them, and indignation against their enemies, called, "The zeal of the Lord of hosts, and his great jealousy."[2] Sometimes it is used for a gracious disposition in man, which has God for its object and so called "zeal towards God." Zeal is again an eager desire after God's glory, and God is the author of this spiritual characteristic, so it is called, "a zeal of God" or "a godly jealousy."[3]

The many kinds of zeal

There are various sorts and kinds of zeal; these kinds must be examined to deduce the right and genuine kind of zeal. Where the true zeal is better known, it may then be better exercised.

Ignorant zeal

First, there is a "zeal of God," which is "not according to knowledge," that the Jews had, as the apostle testifies in Romans 10:2. This was a zealous concern for the performance

---

[2] Isaiah 9:7; Zechariah 1:14; 8:2.
[3] 2 Corinthians 11:2.

of legal duties, and a studious attempt to set them up, and establish them as a justifying righteousness before God; so, it was to the entire neglect and rejection of the righteousness of Christ. Such a zeal arose from ignorance of the perfection of God's righteousness. Yet God's perfect righteousness is displayed in all his ways and works, and he is the judge of the whole earth, and will do right. He will not clear the guilty without full satisfaction to his justice. He will not justify any without a perfect righteousness. God's "judgment of things is according to truth,"[4] he cannot reckon an imperfect righteousness as perfect, or account anything righteous unless it is actually righteous. To secure his honour and glory in this point of accepting only that which is of perfect righteousness, he has set forth Christ to be the propitiatory sacrifice for sin, thereby making satisfaction for it. Only this sacrifice alone was "to declare his righteousness," but of this the legal zealot is ignorant and therefore takes a wrong course.[5]

This worldly zeal arises from ignorance of the righteousness which God requires from the law. The law is holy, just,

---

4   Romans 2:2.
5   Romans 3:26.

and good, and requires a perfect righteousness, both as to the matter of it, and the manner of its performance. All that the law has commanded must be done, precisely according to how it is laid out, or it is of no righteousness. The law is spiritual, and reaches to the heart, the spirit, and the soul of man.[6] The law forbids sinful thoughts, inward lusts, and irregular affections, as well as the outward and grosser sins of life. It allows of no trifling, or little sins, but condemns all. The Pharisee is so ignorant of the true nature of the law that he fails to understand both its extensiveness as well as its spirituality. By such ignorance he sets up his own righteousness as sufficient, and zealously endeavors to establish it but it will be of no service.[7]

This ignorant zeal arises from a want of knowledge of the righteousness of God revealed in the gospel, which is none other than the righteousness of Christ, who is God as well as man. Being ignorant of the righteousness of Christ, his excellency, fullness, and suitableness, men fail to submit to it but reject it, stumbling at the stumbling stone and rock

---

[6] Deuteronomy 6:25.
[7] Matthew 5:19–20.

of offence.[8]

This false zeal arises from an ignorant estimation of their own righteousness. They continue in this ignorance because the Spirit of God has not convinced them of how imperfect and polluted they are, and how their righteousness is not a fit answer to the law of God. They remain short of its demands and requirements, as their own righteousness is insufficient to justify them before God. Though this is the case, they are warmly attached to their own righteousness, and zealous to establish it. But were they to be made sensible of the imperfection and unprofitableness of it, they will surely desire to be found in Christ, and in his righteousness and not their own.[9]

Again, this type of zeal arises from a want of faith in Christ; being destitute of that, these zealots follow eagerly after righteousness but do not attain it, "Because they seek it not by faith, but as it were by the works of the law."[10] Now, what is not of faith is sin, and therefore zeal without

---

8 Romans 1:17; 3:21–22.
9 Philippians 3:9.
10 Romans 9:32. See also John Bunyan, "No way to Heaven but Jesus Christ," in *The Works of that eminent servant of Christ, Mr. John Bunyan*, vol. 3, 4th ed. (Edinburgh: Sands, Murray, and Cochran, 1769), 288.

faith cannot be right. Zeal without faith in Christ is without knowledge. Without the knowledge of Christ, a man is without the knowledge of God in Christ, and therefore he cannot be well pleasing and acceptable to God. This is the kind of ignorant zeal—lacking true righteousness—that these zealots are following and endeavoring to establish.

Such a zealot above described is contrary to the will and way of God, that is, the way he justifies sinners. His zeal must be a false one who seeks justification apart from Christ alone. God has declared his will that a man is not and cannot be justified in the sight of God by the deeds of the law, but that a man is justified by faith in the righteousness of Christ without the deeds of the law. The way and method God takes to justify men is by grace, freely imputing righteousness to them. God makes and accounts them righteous through the obedience and righteousness of his Son.[11] Therefore it must be a blind, ignorant zeal, which sets up a man's post by God's post, and advances his own righteousness above that of Christ's.

---

11   Romans 3:20, 24, 28; 4:6; 5:9.

Mistaken zeal

Second, there is a mistaken zeal for the glory of God. This mistaken zeal is observed when what is right is opposed under a false notion of being contrary to the glory of God. The Bible demonstrates this when Joshua requested of Moses to forbid the young men of prophesying in the camp. Joshua thought such prophesying was neither for the glory of God or to the honour of Moses. We see it most clearly in the Gospels when the priests and scribes were sorely displeased at the children in the temple for crying "hosanna" to the Son of David. Again, we see these characters exhibiting mistaken zeal when they exclaimed against the works of Christ done on the sabbath day, as if his performance was contrary to the honour of the sabbath, the proper sanctification of it, and the glory of God in it. Such was the indiscreet zeal of Peter when he chided Christ for saying he must suffer many things, as if it was injurious to his honour and glory when all these things were right.

This mistaken zeal is shown when that which is not for the glory of God, is wrongly thought to be so and is zealously pursued. The zeal of the idolatrous Gentiles for their idols and idol worship proves a mistaken zeal. The zeal of the Jews for the traditions of the elders, of which the apostle Paul was very zealous before conversion, proves a mistaken zeal. The zeal of the believing Jews in the New Testament who were zealous for continuing the ceremonies of the law, though abrogated, proves to be mistaken zeal.[12] And lastly, the zeal of the Papists for their worship of images, angels, and departed saints—along many other false teachings—is a mistaken zeal.

When improper ways and methods are taken to defend and promote the glory of God then a mistaken zeal has been born into practice. When the disciples, in their zeal for the honour of Christ, sought for fire to come down from heaven upon those who had shown some disrespect to Christ, they were experiencing a mistaken zeal. When Peter, in his preposterous zeal, drew his sword in defense of his master, and cut off the ear of the high priest's servant—for which both the one and the other were rebuked by Christ—we understand Peter had a mistaken zeal.[13]

---

12 Galatians 1:14; Acts 21:20.
13 Luke 9:55; Matthew 26:51.

Superstitious zeal

Third, there is a superstitious zeal like that of the Baal worshippers, who cut themselves with knives and lancets while calling upon their gods. This superstition is in all idolaters as they use a multitude of rites for which they are extremely zealous. The Bible particularly looks to the Athenians who were wholly given to idolatry, and whose city was full of idols, of whom the apostle says that he perceived they "were in all things too superstitious."[14] Because they feared they might be defective in any one aspect of their worship, they exercised caution to the point of erecting an altar to an unknown God so they might be sure to comprehend all. The Jews were little different to the Gentiles in false or mistaken zeal. They were zealous of the traditions of their fathers and were superstitiously careful that they did not eat with unwashed hands, they even paid close attention to the washing of their cups and pots.

Persecuting zeal

Fourth, there is a persecuting zeal under a pretense of the

---

14   Acts 17:22.

glory of God. Before his conversion, Paul says of himself, "concerning zeal, persecuting the church;"[15] that is, he showed his zeal for the glory of God by his persecution of the church of Christ—he made havoc of it. He seems to have respect to this when he tells the Jews that he was "zealous for God, as all of you are this day."[16] In the same way, the "devout and honorable women,"[17] whom the Jews stirred up to persecute the apostles, were no doubt under the influence of such a false zeal. They imagined that what they did was for the glory of God and the honor of religion.

Hypocritical zeal

Fifth, there is a hypocritical zeal for God. We see this portrayed in Jehu when he said, "Come with me, and see my zeal for the Lord."[18] Yet he took no heed to walk in the law of the Lord, and he did not depart from the sins of Jeroboam.[19] Though he destroyed the images of Baal, he still worshipped the calves at Dan and Bethel. Hypocritical zeal is shown in

---

15 Philippians 3:6.
16 Acts 22:3.
17 Acts 13:50.
18 2 Kings 10:16.
19 1 Kings 12:29–31.

the scribes and Pharisees who brought the woman taken in adultery to Christ under a pretense of great regard for the law.[20] Yet these men were guilty of like sins. Judas pretended to have regard for the poor, but only sought to gratify his covetousness.[21] The Pharisees made a show of great zeal for piety by their long prayers, but only sought to devour widows' houses by that same means.[22]

Contentious zeal

Sixth, there is a contentious zeal, which often gives great trouble to Christian communities. This is the zeal of men the apostle speaks of in 2 Timothy 2:14–18 when he says, "If any man seems to be contentious," about trivial matters, things indifferent, and of no moment, "we have no such custom, nor the churches of God," and such things should not be indulged. This sort of zeal is oftentimes no other than a mere argument about words, "a striving about words to no profit." It is a contention about "foolish and unlearned questions," which "engenders strife," and at best brings

---

20   John 8:3, 9.
21   John 12:5–6.
22   Matthew 23:14.

division over things curious and useless. True zeal, on the other hand, is always employed about the more solid and substantial doctrines of the gospel, and the ordinances of Christ.

Temporary zeal

Seventh, sometimes the zeal experienced is only a temporary passion, a flash of zeal that does not continue for long. While Jehoiada the priest lived, Joash did what was right and showed zeal in repairing the house of God. However, after Jehoiada's death, Joash left the house of the Lord God of his fathers and served groves and idols. John the Baptist was a burning and shining light, and his hearers and disciples burned with zeal for him, his ministry, and baptism. Some of these followers grew increasingly passionate concerning their interest of Christ, but it was for a season they "rejoiced in his light." The Galatians were zealously afflicted towards the apostle Paul, to such a degree that they would have been willing to have "plucked out their eyes"[23] and given them to him when they first received him. So acceptable was Paul's

---

23   Galatians 4:15.

ministry to them that they received him as an angel of God, even as Jesus Christ, yet he became their enemy because of his preaching the same truths beyond this early season.

True zeal

Eighth, true zeal is no other than a fervent, ardent love to God and Christ, with a warm concern for their honour and glory. Those who are truly zealous for the Lord of Hosts love him with all their heart, with all their soul, and with all their strength. Those with true zeal love one another fervently because they love the Lord Jesus Christ in sincerity. True zeal is accompanied with a saving knowledge of God and Christ, of God in Christ, and of Christ and him crucified. These believers prefer the excellency of the knowledge of Christ above all other things and prefer him to all created beings—they have faith in God, and in Christ.[24] True faith works by love, and this love constrains them and inspires them with zeal to seek their honour and glory. Whatever they do, whether in things civil or religious, they do all to the glory of God. True zeal must consist of spiritual

---

24   Philippians 3:8; Psalm 73:25.

knowledge, unfeigned faith, and undissembled love.

Zeal is opposed to a neutral spirit in religion, to a halting between two opinions, as this is condemned by Elijah in the Jews.[25] There can be no true zeal for the truth as concerns worship, doctrines, and ordinances, if there is no stability. True zeal is completely contrary to any wavering and inconstancy. Zeal is opposed to carelessness and indifference about religious matters, as witnessed in the Jews of old, when they regarded their own paneled houses but not the house of God. He is a careless man who minds secular affairs more than the interest of religion. Such irreligious men are shown the church of God, the truths of the gospel, and the ordinances of Christ, yet they care for none of these things. True zeal is opposed to such lukewarmness with respect to divine and spiritual things; the Laodicean church was charged with these things, and bore the resentment of Christ.[26]

The objects of zeal

Having considered many false kinds of zeal and demonstrations that are contrary to the will of God in Scripture, and

---

25 1 Kings 18:21.
26 Revelation 3:15–16.

shown at last the true zeal of a believer, let us discern the objects of true zeal.

God

The most obvious object of true zeal is zeal for God. So foundational is this object of faith that false zeal still claims, "a zeal towards God"—even that which is not according to knowledge is said to be "a zeal of God." If Jehu called his hypocritical zeal a "zeal for the Lord," then true zeal most deservedly bears this name. Phinehas had the covenant of an everlasting priesthood given him because he was "zealous for his God,"[27] which springs from a principle of love to God, and its end is his glory. True zeal has for its objects the worship of God, the word of God, and the truths contained in it.

Worship cannot be performed rightly without a knowledge of the God who is worshipped, and his design for worship. The Samaritans did not know who or what they worshipped. The Athenians erected an altar to an unknown God. Though both the Samaritans and Athenians were

---

27   Numbers 25:13.

zealous for worship, their zeal was not according to knowledge. True believers worship God "in the Spirit" because they know him in a spiritual way through faith in Christ, and such a knowledge carries a zealous concern for his glory. These believers worship God in truth and keep close to the pattern of worship he has shown them; they are zealously attached, and will not depart from it.

The word of God is the object of the true believer's zeal. They appeal to the law and to the testimony for the truth of all they say and do. They make Scripture the standard of their faith and practice, and the rule of their worship. They earnestly contend for the perfection and integrity of Scripture, and endeavor with all their might to preserve it as it stands pure and incorrupt.[28]

In similar fashion, true believers are zealous for all those truths contained in God's word. They who have a true zeal are valiant for the truth and can do nothing against it. Rather, they pursue everything for the sake of it, in defense of it, and for the continuance of it. Faithful believers will buy the truth no matter how great the price, and forever esteem its

---

28 2 Corinthians 2:17.

high value. Once held in them, they will not sell it, nor part with it for any price.

The cause of Christ

Another object of zeal is the cause of Christ. As the cause of Christ is the ultimate good, the apostle says, "It is always good to be zealously affected in a good thing."[29] Those who are possessed of this zealous affection do not seek their own ambitions but those of Christ. They have a natural care, as Timothy had, for the state of the church, an interest of Christ and true religion, and a desire for the support of the church's mission. Those affected for the good things of Christ are not only with those particular ministries to which they belong but are zealous to see others make much of Christ. We see that the Corinthian church was not only zealous for their own welfare, but for that of other churches. The apostle testifies that their zeal in their liberal ministration to the saints, had "provoked very many" to the cause of Christ.[30] True zeal for the cause of Christ is concerned with the gospel of Christ, the ordinances of Christ, and the

---

29 Galatians 4:18. Modified from NKJV.
30 2 Corinthians 9:2.

discipline of his house.

There is great reason to be zealous for the gospel of Christ. It is "the gospel of the grace of God," which displays the free grace of God in every part of our salvation. On such a basis, the apostle was so zealously concerned for the gospel of Christ as not to count his life dear to himself, but rather finish his course with joy by bearing a testimony to the gospel. The "gospel of salvation" publishes salvation by Christ by declaring that whoever believes in him will be saved. Because it is, "the gospel of peace," and therefore preaching peace by Jesus Christ; this peace comes only by the blood of his cross. In this gospel of peace the forgiveness of sin is preached in the name of Christ, and justification by his righteousness.

The cause of Christ includes the ordinances of Christ, for which every true Christian should be zealous. Such a zeal includes an enthusiasm to keep the ordinances of the church as they were first delivered, without any innovation or corruption. Zeal for the ordinances also concerns the mode of administration of both baptism and the Lord's Supper in that they should be strictly adhered to. True zeal is demonstrated when only believers in Christ, or such who profess faith in him, are admitted to these ordinances.

The discipline of Christ's house should be the object of our zeal, as it was of his who said the "zeal of your house has consumed me."[31] This is shown when the rules of discipline are strictly observed, both with respect to private and public offences. Such a discipline for the church may look like the example of Ephesus when the members of a local body "will not tolerate evil people"[32] to continue with them in fellowship. Whether men of immoral lives, or those who have drank false doctrines, the true house of Christ will withdraw from those who walk a disordered path and reject those who refuse sound faith.

Against all false worship

True zeal is also expressed against all false worship, particularly idolatry—having more than one God. This zeal may be found stirred in those who live among the heathens, or even those who bear the name of Christian. We look to Moses, as when his anger, zeal, and indignation burned hot against the Israelites for their idolatrous worship of the calf. He

---

31 Psalm 69:9.
32 Revelation 2:2.

demonstrated this zeal when he broke the tables of the law which were in his hands, and then he ordered the Levites to take up swords and slay every man his brother, companion, and neighbor. We remember how jealous Elijah was for the Lord God of hosts because Israel had forsaken the covenant of the Lord, had thrown down his altar, and slain his prophets. Where there is true love for God, and zeal for his worship, there will be hatred of every false way, no matter the shape.

Zeal shows itself against all errors in doctrine, with special affection for the persons of the Trinity: Father, Son, and Spirit. True believers will show a zeal for the fundamental doctrines of religion and against all error that may come against these truths. Those who deny right doctrine are to be rebuked sharply, warmly, vehemently, and with a becoming zeal that they may be won to sound faith. Those who do not bring the doctrine of Christ respecting his person, office, and grace, are not to be received into the house of the saints or to be bid God-speed.

Christian zeal comes against all immorality in practice. True zeal will be as much levelled against a man's own sins as against the sins of others. He will be concerned to remove the beam out of his own eye, as well as the mote out of his brother's eye. He will be severe against his own right hand or right eye sins, such a zealousness proven even against his own dear flesh. This zeal against immorality will manifest as real godly sorrow for sin, and true repentance to salvation. The Christian must be diligent to as "What zeal is stirring in you against your sin?" And just as well "What zeal is stirring in you against another's sin?" But zeal against the sins of another must be tempered with commiseration and pity to the sinner.[33]

Duties of religion and service
True zeal is concerned in all the duties of religion and is demonstrated through them. Zeal should lead to a zealous, warm, and fervent in spirit in such a manner of serving the Lord. True zeal could never lead a believer to ministry a gospel duty in a cold, indifferent way. It is said of Apollos, that he was "fervent in spirit when he spoke and taught diligently the things of the Lord," that is those doctrines of the gospel with which he was then acquainted.[34]

---

33 2 Corinthians 7:11; 12:21.
34 Acts 18:25; Romans 12:11.

Zeal is also required in prayer to God; just as Epaphras was always "laboring fervently in prayers"[35] for the church at Colossae. Likewise, we know that it is the "fervent prayer" of the righteous man that is effectual.[36] This same zeal should be shown in the love of the saints to one another.[37]

In short, believers in Christ ought to be "zealous of good works,"[38] careful to maintain them, diligent in the performance of them, especially of those which are the greater and weightier duties of religion—even still, believers should not neglect or omit those lesser duties.

According to the duty of gospel ministry, good men are the objects of this true zeal. When the apostle Paul was informed of the "fervent mind" or zeal of the Corinthians towards him—of the warm love and ardent affection they had for him—he then advised them to covet earnestly, to desire the best gifts, spiritual ones, fitting for public service, even prophecy, or preaching.[39]

---

35 Colossians 4:12.
36 James 5:16.
37 1 Peter 1:22; 4:8.
38 Titus 2:14.
39 1 Corinthians 12:31; 14:1, 12, 39; 2 Corinthians 7:7.

Motivations for true zeal

The example of Christ, whom David prophetically represented saying, "zeal for your house consumes me,"[40] showed true zeal as consuming his spirits, his strength, and life, so by this zeal he exerted himself in his public ministrations. He showed his zeal for the doctrines of the gospel, by his warm and constant preaching, even with power and authority, in a manner by which the scribes and Pharisees did not. Through this zeal he took indefatigable pains in ministry, travelling from place to place, running the risk of his life, and exposing himself to frequent dangers on that account. Zeal erupted from Christ for the worship of the house of God, as appears by railing[41] so severely against the traditions of men. Christ shows the example of this zeal by asserting the purity of worship in spirit and in truth; expressing his resentment at the profanation of the house of God, while driving out the buyers and sellers from it. This zeal brought the abovementioned Psalm to the minds of the disciples, who clearly discerned the fulfilment of it.

The zeal of Christ against immorality was seen also in his

---

40 Psalm 69:9; John 2:17.
41 Inveighing.

sharp reproofs of the vices of the age, both in professors and profane; and in all he is a pattern worthy of our imitation.

True zeal answers a principal end of redemption by Christ, yet the claim to redemption seems precarious for those who have no zeal for God or any zeal to obey that which he desires.[42] The love of Christ in redeeming his people will constrain them to show a zeal for his glory, both with respect to doctrine and practice.

It is "good," the apostle says, "to be zealously affected for"[43] what is good, and what is approved and commended by Christ. The church at Ephesus was zealous in this way because she could not bear those who were evil and contrary to remain with them as one body. The Ephesian church disapproved and resented any sort of lukewarmness. Yet the church of Laodicea was at the same time threatened to be unchurched for lukewarmness and was therefore strongly exhorted to be "zealous and repent."[44] A lukewarm temper, which is the opposite to zeal, is inconsistent with true religion, which has always life and heat in it, but to be neither

---

42 Titus 2:14.
43 Galatians 4:18.
44 Revelation 3:15–16, 19–20.

"cold nor hot" is condemned as having no religion at all.

The zeal of persons shown in a false way should stimulate those professing our true religion to show at least an equal zeal. We know that "all people will walk everyone in the name of his god," and appear zealous for his worship, but "we will walk in the name of the Lord our God," at least we ought to do so, and determine upon it.[45] The Pharisees showed great zeal and endured great hardships in crossing land and sea just to make one proselyte and did so to make a man worse than he was to start, even worse than the Pharisees.[46] Should we Christians not exert ourselves to the uttermost for the interest of the Redeemer? This must be a becoming zeal. And in order to keep up and promote such zeal, it will be proper frequently to meditate on the love of God and Christ, the blessings of the gospel of the grace of God, the excellency of the Christian religion, the benefits and privileges of the house of God, to converse often with warm and lively Christians, and to sit under a savory and fervent ministry.

---

45 Micah 4:5
46 Matthew 23:15.

THREE

The fear of God

The fear of God has so great a concern in divine worship that the phrase is sometimes used as the whole of worship. A worshipper of God is frequently described in Scripture as one that fears him. This phrase is particularly used concerning internal or experimental worship as distinguished from an external observance of the divine commands. According to the wise man, the whole of experimental and practical religion lies in these two things, to "fear God and keep his commandments."[1] The whole of worship is expressed as the fear of God, so the way it is to be performed is directed to be in fear and with fear. God is to be served "with reverence

---

1 Ecclesiastes 12:13.

and godly fear."[2]

God alone is the object of fear

There is a fear due to men, "fear to whom fear is due;" that is, fear should be rendered to whom it is due.[3] There is a fear and reverence due to parents from their children,[4] which is shown by the honour and respect paid to them, and the obedience yielded to them.[5] The argument from here is strong to the fear and reverence of God the Father of spirits.[6] There is a fear and reverence in the conjugal state due from wives to their husbands.[7] The marital relation affords a reason and argument why the church should fear and serve the Lord her God because he is her husband.[8] There is a fear and reverence that servants should show to their masters,[9] and if such masters are to be obeyed with fear, then much more our Master who is in heaven. This is the same argument the

2 Psalm 2:11; 5:7; 89:7; Hebrews 12:28.
3 Romans 13:7.
4 Leviticus 19:3; Hebrews 12:9.
5 Ephesians 6:1–2.
6 Hebrews 12:9; 1 Peter 1:14, 17.
7 Ephesians 5:33; 1 Peter 3:5–6.
8 Psalm 45:11.
9 Ephesians 6:5.

Lord himself uses: "If I am a master, then where is my reverence?"[10] There is a fear and reverence which ministers of the word should receive by those to whom they minister;[11] this is one part of that double honour they are worthy of for the sake of their work. Herod, though a wicked man, "feared John;" he did not dread him but respected him and so gladly listened to him.[12]

There is a fear and reverence to be rendered to magistrates and especially to the king, the chief magistrate.[13] If an earthly king is to be feared and reverenced, much more the King of Kings and Lord of Lords, "Who would not fear you, O king of nations?"[14] But then men are not so to be feared by the people of God, let them be in what character, relation, and station secret, as to be deterred by them from the service of God. However, the people of God are not to be fearful of men so to be hindered from serving the one true God—a fear of man too often brings a snare in this respect. The Christian is to be steadfast in character, relation,

---

10 Malachi 1:6.
11 1 Samuel 12:18.
12 Mark 6:20.
13 Proverbs 24:21; Romans 13:7.
14 Jeremiah 10:7.

and station with regard to fearing God first. God is to be listened to, served, and obeyed rather than men of the highest class and rank. The God-fearer is not to be afraid of losing his favor and esteem or of gaining the ill will of worldly men. Remember, there were Pharisees who were convinced that Jesus was the Christ, but would not confess him as such because they were more afraid of being put out of the synagogues and losing the love and praise of men than of honouring God.

Believers should not be afraid of the scorn and reproaches of men or be intimidated from serving the Lord their God. With Moses, believers should esteem the reproaches of men as for the Lord's sake—as greater riches than the treasures of Egypt. They should not be frightened from their profession of religion or from keeping attention to it by the threats and menaces of men or by all the persecution they may endure from their abusers. Those who can kill the body are not to be feared, but God is to be feared who can destroy both body and soul in hell.[15] Those who fear men and so neglect the worship of God are truly to be fearful

---

15 Matthew 10:28.

because they will have their part in the lake of fire and brimstone.[16]

If God is on the side of his people—and he most certainly is—they have no reason to fear what man can do to them. God only is the object of fear: "You shall fear the Lord your God, and serve him," that is, him only. This is the principal thing God requires of his people, and they are bound in duty to render fear to him. "Now, O Israel, what does the Lord your God require of you, but to fear the Lord your God?"[17] This is the first thing, and all other commands follow it. Because he is the object of fear for good men, he is called *fear* itself,[18] which is evidenced in the name "fear of Isaac"[19] when in place of the God of Isaac by whom Jacob swore.[20] The Chaldeans paraphrase the word *fear* as it is sometimes used in place of the true God as well as used of idols. The Greek word for *God* is even derived from *fear* and from this it was that the Lacedemonians worshipped *fear* as a deity, and had a temple for Pavor and Pallor, that is,

---

16 Revelation 21:8.
17 Deuteronomy 6:13; 10:20.
18 Deuteronomy 10:12.
19 Genesis 31:42.
20 Genesis 31:53.

fearfulness and *paleness*, as mentioned among the Romans by Tullus Hostilius (710–641 BC). Yet to believers, none but the true God is the object of fear.

God's name and nature

God is to be feared because of his name and nature. Scripture reads, "Holy and reverend is his name,"[21] particularly his name Jehovah as it is expressive of his essence and nature. His name is particular to him "that you may fear this fearful and glorious name, The Lord your God."[22] There is no other name that is to be feared except the name of God; his name commonly spoken in Scripture ought always to be used in a revered manner. It must never be used with slight and trivial occasion or with great irreverence as happens too often when men are so frequently apt to say, O Lord! O God! Good God! Those men who profess the fear of God especially should be careful of such language, for it is nothing other than taking the name of God in vain.

---

21 Deuteronomy 28:58.
22 Psalm 112:9.

God in three persons

God is to be feared not only in essence but in persons, as God the Father, God the Son, and God the Holy Spirit. It is said of the Jews in the latter day that they will "seek the Lord their God, and David their king, and will fear the Lord and his goodness in the latter days."[23] In this future time, the Lord, Jehovah the Father and all his goodness, will be feared by them as distinguished from the Messiah the Son of God, and David their king, who will be sought for by them. Likewise, it is said in Malachi 4:2, "To you that fear my name," that is Jehovah is the name of the Lord of Hosts. Yet it is also mentioned that "the Sun of righteousness will arise with healing in his wings."[24] This is the Son of God, who is the brightness of his Father's glory, the express image of his person, and so distinguished from him whose name is feared.

Jehovah the Son is also the object of divine fear and reverence. Scripture says, "Let him be your fear, and let him be your dread;"[25] that is, let the Son be the object of your

---

23 Hosea 3:5.
24 Malachi 4:2.
25 Isaiah 8:13.

fear and reverence. The divine person, the Son, "will be a sanctuary" to worship in, and a place of refuge for his people in times of distress. Yet the second person of the Trinity will be "a stone of stumbling, and a rock of offence,"[26] which are phrases applied to Christ and can only be said of him. When Jehovah the Father, the Lord of the vineyard, sent away many of his ill-treated servants he says, "I will send my beloved Son," meaning Christ, the only begotten Son of the Father. In sending him, the Father says, "perhaps they will reverence him when they see him," they ought to have done so.[27] Reverence should be given to the heir of the vineyard, the Son of God, his church, and those homes of believers who reverence him.

Jehovah the Spirit is also the object of fear. The Israelites in the wilderness rebelled against him, vexed him, and they smarted for it—the Spirit of God "turned to be their enemy, and fought against them."[28] Because they lied to the Holy Spirit, which was a most irreverent treatment of him, Ananias and Sapphira were punished with death. The saints

---

26   Isaiah 8:13–14; Romans 9:32–33; 1 Peter 2:7–8.
27   Luke 20:13.
28   Isaiah 63:10.

should be careful that they do not grieve the Holy Spirit by their unbecoming conduct toward him from whom they receive many blessings and favours.

God's perfection

God is the object of fear; and this on account of his perfections. God should be feared according to his majesty and greatness in general, as he is clothed with majesty—majesty and honour are ever before him. As Scripture states, "with him is terrible majesty,"[29] such is sufficient to command an awe of him. God is to be feared for his omnipotence, for "he is excellent in power,"[30] as well as for his omniscience because nothing can be hidden from his sight.

The most enormous actions committed in the dark are seen by him with whom the darkness and the light are alike. His omnipresence should bring a worshipful fear for he fills heaven and earth and there is no fleeing from him. It may be added, the justice and holiness of God, which make his majesty the more terrible and to be revered, since he is not only excellent in power but also "in judgment, and in plenty of

---

29 Job 37:22.
30 Job 37:23.

justice."[31] Truly it is a fearful thing to fall into the hands of a just and sin-avenging God, "the living God, the everlasting King, at whose wrath and indignation the nations tremble, and are not able to bear."[32]

God's works

The works of God reveal him to be a proper object of fear and reverence. The Psalmist considers God's work of creation: "Let all the earth fear the Lord, let all the inhabitants of the world stand in awe of him."[33] God has made such a display of his greatness and goodness in these marvelous works for the purpose of showing his own worthiness of fear and reverence. Even those things that may seem small are yet enough to command awe and wonder, even fear of God. The prophet regards the divine, "Do you not fear me? declares the Lord. Do you not tremble before me? I have placed the sand as the boundary for the sea, a perpetual barrier that it cannot pass."[34] Even though God was displaying

---

31   Job 37:23. Gill also cites 2 Chronicles 19:7 in conjunction with this reference.
32   Jeremiah 10:10.
33   Psalm 33:8.
34   Jeremiah 5:22.

the goodness of his providence through these works, the people's stupidity and lack of fear and reverence is on full display.

Jeremiah records, "They do not say in their hearts, 'Let us fear the Lord our God, who gives the rain in its season, the autumn rain and the spring rain, and keeps for us the weeks appointed for the harvest.'"[35] Though these are common providential blessings, yet they should engage men to fear the Lord and his goodness.

Men should especially consider God's works of grace. Such a consideration should produce an effect upon the hearts of his people as these works are nothing less than divine power. God's pardoning grace and mercy are truly objects of fear as it is clearly shown: "with you there is forgiveness that you may be feared."[36]

God's judgments

The judgments of God which he threatens and sometimes inflicts, and the promises of grace he makes and always fulfils, render him an object of fear and reverence. The

---

35 Jeremiah 5:24.
36 Psalm 130:4; Hosea 3:5.

judgments of God on sinners are awful to the saints and strike their minds with fear of God. Even David cries, "My flesh trembles for fear of you and I am afraid of your Judgments,"[37] and this not regarding afflictions upon himself but as terrible sufferings befalling others. God's judgments are dreadful and formidable to sinners when they see them near approaching. Sinners flee to the holes and clefts of rocks and into the caves for fear of the Lord, "and from the splendor of his majesty, when he rises terrify the earth."[38] Nothing has a greater influence on a filial and godly fear in the saints—to stir them up to the exercise of this fear—than the free, absolute, and unconditional promises of grace in the covenant. Thus, after the apostle had observed these promises, he strongly urges perfecting holiness in the fear of God.[39]

The natures and kinds of fear

There are a multitude of kinds of fear that humans experience. There are many false ways to experience or exercise fear, and many of these natures and kinds of fear are not

---

37 Psalm 119:120.
38 Isaiah 2:19, 21.
39 2 Corinthians 6:16, 18; 7:1.

biblical, reverential, or right as according to holy Scripture. Therefore, various kinds of fear will be observed here in effort to discern the right, godly fear.

Superstitious fear

There is a fear which is not good or commendable, and it shows itself in different forms. There is an idolatrous and superstitious fear, which is called a fear of demons, to which the whole city of Athens was greatly addicted. This was observed in them by the apostle when to their disgrace he said, "I perceive that in all things you are too superstitious,"[40] because they were given to the fear and worship of false deities. Such is all worship that springs up from a man's own will. All worship not founded in the word of God necessarily brings forth a spirit of bondage and fear. All such false and vain imaginations as idolatrous worship only inject dread and terror into the minds of men and cause them to "fear where no fear is,"[41] or where there is no reason for fear. This worship is observed in the pains of purgatory after death, which was invented by the Papists to extort money from

---

40 Acts 17:22.
41 Psalm 53:5.

men. Such false worship is likewise seen in the imagination of the Jews who will beat a dead body as it descends into the grave.

External fear

There is an external fear of God, an outward show and profession of it which is nothing more than idolatrous fear. This outward show was taught by the precepts of men, like those of Samaria who pretended to fear the Lord as the priest instructed them and yet served their own gods. Job's friends supposed that all he had was an external fear of the true God and that he was punished for casting off that.[42]

Hypocritical fear

There is a hypocritical fear, exposed when men draw near to God with their mouths and honor him with their lips, yet their hearts are far from him. Such is the case when men fear and serve God for some sinister end and selfish view. Satan insinuated that this was the case with Job, "Does Job fear God for nothing?"[43] The same insinuation is suggested by

42 Job 15:4.
43 Job 1:9.

Eliphaz, "Is not this your fear?"[44]

Servile fear

There is a servile fear which is not a right fear of God. This is a kind of fear that some servants have toward their masters which is not from love but from fear of punishment. The Jews subjected themselves to this kind of fear under the legal dispensation, as it was called to them a "spirit of bondage to fear." Now that the saints are "delivered out of the hands" of sin, Satan, and the law, they "serve" the Lord "without fear," without slavish fear but with a filial fear instead.[45]

Idolatrous fear

Idolatrous fear is a sense and guilt of sin on the conscience without a view of pardon. As soon as Adam and Eve were sensible of their sin and nakedness they fled from the presence of God and hid themselves among the trees of the garden; this because they had as yet no understanding of pardoning grace. Adam responded to God calling for him, "I heard your voice in the garden, and I was afraid because

---

44 Job 4:6.
45 Romans 8:15; Luke 1:74–75.

I was naked, and I hid myself."[46] A wicked man who is conscious of his guilt will flee when no one pursues. He is like Pashur, who was a "fear round about" and a terror to himself and others.

When the law enters the conscience of a sinner and wages war upon the sinner, this leads to an idolatrous fear. When the law comes with powerful convictions of sin, and with menaces of punishment for it, a sense and present wrath over sin will fill their conscience and leave a fearful perspective on coming judgment. God's judgment is nothing less than a "fiery indignation" which will consume all God's adversaries. Idolatrous fear comes upon those in a condition of sin and leads them to long for rocks and mountains to fall on them and hide them from the wrath of God—to stand before the Creator appears to them so intolerable.

The curse of the law and the weight of it on the conscience comes out of an idolatrous fear. The voice of the law is terrible, and when that voice is heard those who hear it plead to hear it no more. The law accuses a person of sin, pronounces guilt on them, and ministers condemnation.

---

46   Genesis 3:10.

The language of conviction is this: "Cursed is everyone who does not abide by all things written in the Book of the Law, and do them."[47] To hear this curse is dreadful when the conscience of a sinner is awakened. How much more terrible is it when a sinner feels all the curses of the law upon him, and yet knows of no means for pardon? What kind of fear strikes the sinner when he hears that, "the anger of the Lord, and his jealousy smoke against" him, "and all the curses written in this book settle upon him;"[48] with what slavish fear must fill him?

A view of death as the demerit of sin comes out of an idolatrous fear. As Scripture states, "The wages of sin is death,"[49] that is, death is the just desert of sin. Sin is the sting of death because sin gives death its venom and fatal influence. It is sin that makes death that terrible thing it is. Some who "through fear of death are all their lifetime subject to bondage,"[50] and are under a continual servile fear of it. A dread of hell and everlasting damnation comes out of this

---

47 Galatians 3:10.
48 Deuteronomy 29:20.
49 Romans 6:23.
50 Hebrews 2:15.

idolatrous fear. This fear is of the same kind as that of the devils' who believe there is one God and tremble. Like these devils, many sinners tremble under their present wrath and future torment. Many wicked men, as with Cain, have a fearful apprehension of everlasting punishment—and it is greater than all they can bear in this life.

Filial fear

There is also fear of God different from this idolatrous fear and very much its opposite. This may be called a family fear, or a filial fear like that of a son to a father—the Scriptures call it godly fear.[51] The same word is used of the fear and reverence of Christ to his divine Father who was "heard in that he feared," or "because of fear."[52] Christ's filial fear toward his Father was fixed on honouring him, in obedience to him, and in submission to his will, even when with fervent prayers he sought pleaded against death. This filial fear arises in the saints.

Based in his work of adoption, God delivers his people out of a servile fear and gives them a family bond—such a

51 Hebrews 12:28.
52 Hebrews 5:7.

filial fear comes through the sonship given in Christ. As the apostle says, "You have not received the spirit of bondage again to fear, but you have received the spirit of adoption, whereby we cry, 'Abba, Father,'"[53] and so are freed. Those who fear the Lord are made relations of him. Because of this relationship they therefore fear him as he takes notice and regards each as one of his own children, given such a sense of this new relationship. The evidence of this relationship seems to be what is implied in Psalm 103:13: "As a father shows compassion to his children, so the Lord shows compassion to those who fear him," where they that fear the Lord in the latter clause answer as children in the former.

This fear comes out of the love of God shed abroad in the heart by the Spirit, which produces love to God. There is no slavish fear with God, but as his child there is a perfect love. There is a sense of the perfect, everlasting, and unchangeable love of God which "casts out"[54] such kind of slavish fear. The true fear of God is no other than a reverential affection for God flowing from a sense of his love. Those who fear him do not dread his wrath, but desire his

---

53 Romans 8:17.
54 1 John 4:18.

presence and more of a communion with him. These are the ones who say, "Whom have I in heaven but you? There is none on earth that I desire besides you."[55]

This filial fear is attended with faith and trust in God. This is a fiducial fear, so it is that those who fear the Lord also trust in him. Fear and trust are here two characters put together and which describe the same persons. Those who fear the Lord are exhorted and encouraged to trust in him.[56] Job was a man that feared God[57] and yet his faith and confidence were such that he could say, "Though he slay me, yet will I trust in him."[58] What a strong expression of faith in Christ as his living Redeemer![59]

Filial fear is a fear that is consistent with great joy in the Lord, as Scripture commands "Serve the Lord with fear, and rejoice with trembling," and with the utmost courage and magnanimity of mind.[60] It is a fearless fear! A man that fears the Lord has no reason to fear anything or what any man or

---

55   Psalm 73:25.
56   Psalm 31:19; 115:11.
57   Job 1:1.
58   Job 13:15.
59   Job 19:25.
60   Psalm 2:11.

devil can do to him. He may say as David did, "The Lord is my light and my salvation, whom shall I fear?"[61]

Such a fear of God is opposed to pride and self-confidence. It is a humble fear, a diffidence of a man's self, placing his trust and hope alone in God. Scripture says, "Be not high minded, but fear."[62] This is the kind of fear and trembling, or modesty and humility, with which the saints are exhorted to work out or employ in themselves as accompanying salvation. Knowing, such as related to "both to will and to do,"[63] is the disposition and ability to perform any duty rightly; this knowing is the efficacious operation of the Spirit of God. It is by the grace of God they are what they are and that they do what they do. Those who fear the Lord "rejoice in Christ Jesus, and have no confidence in the flesh,"[64] declaring that when they have done all they can they are but unprofitable servants.

---

61 Psalm 27:1, 3.
62 Romans 11:20.
63 Philippians 2.12–13.
64 Philippians 3:3.

Fear of God manifested

Acknowledging the various kinds of fear a person may experience in this life, a believer may be sure of the gifted fear of God by discerning certain manifestations of such a fear. The following examples of such useful, sanctifying fear may be discerned according to a right fear of God.

Hatred of sin

Fear of God is manifested in a hatred of sin. "The fear of the Lord is to hate evil,"[65] as nothing is more opposite to good than evil, so nothing is more to be abhorred. Sin is to be hated with a Stygian hatred as of hating hell itself, "abhor that which is evil."[66] A man that fears God, who has a reverential affection for him, will hate sin as being contrary to him: "You who love the Lord, hate evil,"[67] everything that is evil is hated by such a man. A godly man will hate his own evil thoughts, which are only evil and that continually. The heart is full of evil thoughts, and they pour out of it daily; these are to be the object of a good man's hatred. David

---

65 Proverbs 8:13.
66 Romans 12:9.
67 Psalm 97:10.

says, "I hate vain thoughts."[68] As only a man is conscious and privy to his own thoughts, his hatred for them shows that the fear of God is in his heart.

Evil words are also hated by the man who fears God. Not only cursing, swearing, blasphemy, and all obscene and filthy language, but every vain and idle word is hated by the godly man. He hates every foolish and frothy expression that comes out of his mouth when not on his guard, as well as all those words that give him uneasiness about being displeasing to God, grieving to his Spirit, and what must be accounted for in the day of judgment. As "in many words" there are "many vanities," the wise man opposes them in the fear of God.[69]

If evil thoughts and evil words are hated by the godly, then most certainly evil actions are to be hated. Not only those of others, as the deeds of the Nicolaitans, and the outward filthy conversations of the wicked, but a man will have hatred for his own actions springing from corrupt nature—those things done by him contrary to the law of his mind. As with Paul, he says, "I do not do what I want, but I

---

68 Psalm 119:113.
69 Ecclesiastes 5:7.

do the very thing I hate."[70] Evil men and their company are abhorrent to those who fear the Lord, and such company is shunned and avoided by them. The man who fears God will choose not to have any fellowship with the unfruitful works of darkness or the workers of such evil. Participating in any fellowship with them is a grief and burden to those who hate sin, as it was to Lot, David, Isaiah, Jeremiah, and others. Truly, such communion was hateful to them: "Do I not hate those who hate you? I hate them with perfect hatred."[71]

All evil and false ways, not only of immorality but of superstition, are rejected with abhorrence by men that fear the Lord and make his word the rule of their faith and practice. Wisdom herself, or Christ, is set as an example to prove the truth of the assertion in "Pride and arrogance, and the way of evil, and perverted speech I hate."[72] Wisdom is justified in her children as David says, who was a child of wisdom, "I hate every false way."[73] Yes, see that all evil doctrines which only serve to corrupt the divine persons in the Godhead,

---

70   Romans 7:15.
71   Psalm 139:21–22; Proverbs 4:14–15.
72   Proverbs 8:13.
73   Psalm 119:128.

the free grace of God in man's salvation, the person and offices of Christ, or the operations of the Spirit, are the object of the hatred and aversion of one that fears God. The godly man cannot bear to hear those who are evil, who corrupt God's true doctrines. He will not even let them into his home or wish them safe travel. In short, everything that is evil in its nature is in every shape exceedingly sinful. Sin is a breach of the law of God, contrary to his nature, and abominable. The God-fearer hates such sin by his very soul. The fear of the Lord is manifested by him who hates sin.

Fleeing evil

Fear of God shows itself through a saint departing from evil, just as Scripture says, "By the fear of the Lord men depart from evil."[74] This departing is not only from open and public sins, but from private and secret ones. Job was a man that feared God and fled from evil, avoided it, and departed from it—as every wise man does. Yes, to depart from evil is understanding; this shows a man both to be a wise man and one that fears the Lord.[75] Yes, a man who fears God will

---

74   Proverbs 16:6; 3:7.
75   Job 1:1; 28:28; Proverbs 14:16.

abstain from all appearance of evil, from everything that looks like it or could lead to it. He will shun every avenue, and every bypath that has a tendency to ensnare him; and so taking the wise man's advice: "Do not enter into the path of the wicked."[76]

Nonconformity to the world
The fear of God is evidenced in those who do not permit themselves to do what others do, or what they themselves formerly did. Speaking of wrongs done by former governors, Nehemiah says, "I did not do these things because of the fear of God."[77] This is not to say that those who fear God are without sin. Job feared God but was not free from sin; however, he was sensible of it, acknowledged it, and sought pardon for it. Those who fear God cannot give themselves the same liberty to sin that other people have. They cannot walk as other Gentiles walk, in the vanity of their minds, and in a sinful course of life. Truly, this is not how they learned Christ, for the grace of God teaches them other things.

---

76 Proverbs 4:14–15.
77 Nehemiah 5:15.

Inoffensive nature

The fear of God manifests itself by a carefulness not to offend God or man. Fear of God introduces in the conscience a mindfulness so to avoid offending either God or neighbor. Those who fear God would willingly avoid giving offence to Jew, Gentile, or the church of God. Next to God, they are careful that they do not offend against the next generation of his children, either by word or deed. They are careful not to put stumbling blocks before any but lead others in the fear the Lord—to do otherwise would be contrary to it.[78] No, these worshipers are not only on their guard to avoid sin by offending others but are in direct opposition to such practice. The spiritual part within these people fights against the carnal part. There are two armies in them fighting one against another; this is how they strive against sin, antagonize it, and take to themselves the whole armor of God.

Constancy of worship

The fear of God in men is seen by a constant attendance

---

78   Leviticus 19:14.

to the worship of God, and by a strict observation of his will. The fear of God is observed to have so great a share and concern in divine worship that the phrase is sometimes used for both internal and external worship on the whole. Those who fear the Lord cannot be lackadaisical about neglecting the worship of God. As his people desire to be filled with the knowledge of his will, so they should be found in the practice of it. Worshipers should be like Zacharias and Elizabeth and walk in all the ordinances and commands of the Lord as blamelessly as they can. They should fear God and keep his commandments as is required of man. Those who make a custom of forsaking the assembly of gathering to worship God have, according to this interpretation, cast off a right fear of God.

Sacrificial spirit

The fear of God is demonstrated in faithful men as they do not withhold anything from God, though it may be ever so dear to them. Whenever the Lord requires something of them, they will render it his own. Abraham shows this when he so readily offered up his son at the command of God. He then received this testimony from God, "Now know I," says the Lord, "that you fear God."[79] It then demonstrates the contrary, when men withhold from God what he expects from them—as in the case of Ananias and Sapphira. This is a proof that the fear of God is not before their eyes much less in their hearts.

Causes of fear of God

Prior to noting other causes, the primary observation drawn from Scripture is that the fear of God is not from nature, and it is not natural in men. The want of such godly fear is a part of the description of corrupt nature. Scripture notes, "There is no fear of God before their eyes."[80] It may be said of the heart of every natural man, just as what Abraham said of Gerar: "Surely the fear of God is not in this place."[81] It is concluded from the wickedness that is in man's heart and what comes out of it. Again, Scripture says, "The transgression of the wicked," is discovered by his words and works, his life and actions. This corruption "speaks within my heart," so this verse shows and speaks as plainly as can be from the

---

79   Genesis 22:12.
80   Romans 3:18.
81   Genesis 20:11.

observation of David, "that there is no fear of God" before a natural man's eyes.[82]

Fear of God is a grace gift

Fear of God is a grace gift granted by him alone. Scripture says, "O that there were such a heart in them that they would fear me," or "who will give such an heart?"[83] No one but God can give a new heart. God has promised this gift in his covenant. It is a blessing of his grace which he has provided through his covenant, "I will give them one heart and one way, that they may fear me forever. I will put my fear in their hearts, that they will not depart from me."[84]

Fear of God comes by the Holy Spirit

Fear of God is implanted in the heart at regeneration. It was never, and could never be in the heart prior to the Spirit of God putting it there. As soon as a man is born again this fear appears even with other graces. During the first moments of conversion there is quickly found a tenderness of conscience

---

82 Psalm 36:1.
83 Deuteronomy 5:29.
84 Jeremiah 32:39–40.

with respect to sin and a carefulness not to offend God. Indeed "the fear of the Lord is the beginning of wisdom," and that includes spiritual wisdom.[85] No man is truly wise until he fears God, and as soon as he fears the Lord he begins to be wise—certainly not before! Yes, the fear of the Lord is wisdom itself and it is that wisdom and truth which God desires and puts into the inward and hidden parts of a man's heart.[86]

Fear of God is grown and strengthened

The word and prayer are the means of attaining the fear of the Lord. This is a duty and expression of worship that all believers must learn. Scripture does not leave anyone out: "Come you children, and listen to me," says David, "I will teach you the fear of the Lord."[87] The law of God, and especially the whole of legal and evangelical doctrine, is the means for learning a right fear of God.[88] Therefore learning God's word and spiritual exercises like prayer are together

---

85 Psalm 111:10; Proverbs 9:10.
86 Job 28:28; Psalm 51:6.
87 Psalm 34:11.
88 Deuteronomy 4:10; 17:19.

called the fear of the Lord.[89] Even so, these means of growing in spiritual diligence, in seeking after and earnestly pursuing God, are a grace gift given by him—such a fear of the Lord is yet union with him to be prayed for.[90] The means for growing in fear of the Lord is encouraged, promoted, and increased by fresh discoveries of the grace and goodness of God, "They will fear the Lord and his goodness."[91] The goodness of God makes known, bestows, and applies, great influences for right fear of him. This is especially true in considering the application of his pardoning grace and mercy, "With you there is forgiveness that you may be feared."[92]

The goodness connected to fear of God

Of all the characteristics by which Scripture describes the people of God, none of them offer more promises of God's goodness towards them than fear of God.

---

[89] Psalm 19:7, 9.
[90] Psalm 86:11; Proverbs 2:3–5.
[91] Hosea 3:5.
[92] Psalm 130:4.

Promises for this life and the life to come

Godliness in general, and fear of the Lord in particular, offer promise in this temporal life and life eternal. There is promise that believers will have no want, even of temporal good things: "O fear the Lord, you his saints, for there is no want to those that fear him,"[93] not of any good thing! These good things are characterized as things suitable and convenient for them, and things of which God in his wisdom sees fit and proper for them at the right time. These are not things that are necessarily asked for, but means by which God will do wonders for his people, and provide open sources of relief they had not thought of.[94]

Though God's people may receive few good things from out of this world, yet "better is a little with the fear of the Lord than great treasure and turmoil with it."[95] A little of this world with the fear of God and his righteousness is far better than great revenues without righteousness and fear of God. Proper fear of God is better than the riches of many

---

93   Psalm 34:9–10.
94   Isaiah 41:17–18; 43:19–20.
95   Proverbs 15:16.

wicked persons.[96] Yes, wealth and riches are promised to be in the house of that man that fears the Lord—what is meant by that is humility and the fear of the Lord are riches, and honour, and life.[97] This truth can only be understood by some, not of all that fear the Lord. Those with a right fear of the Lord will understand that spiritual wealth, riches, honour, and life are intended, since the fear of the Lord itself is the good man's treasure. Fear of the Lord is a treasure of itself.[98]

It is said that the man that fears the Lord will eat of the labour of his hands, and he will not only be happy and well with him in his person, but in his whole family. His wife will be as a fruitful vine by the sides of his house, and his children will be as olive plants round about his table.[99]

Those who fear the Lord are in the utmost safety. Those who fear the Lord have a strong confidence on which they depend, therefore they have no reason to be afraid of anything else. The angel of the Lord encompasses them,

---

96   Psalm 37:16; Proverbs 16:8.
97   Psalm 112:1, 3; Proverbs 22:4.
98   Isaiah 33:6.
99   Psalm 128:1–4.

protects them, defends them, and delivers them from danger, all enemies, and keeps evil from visiting them.[100] Yes, the fear of the Lord prolongs their days, and even adds to them as a great temporal blessing.[101] The wise man says of a sinner that though their days are long, yet they will not be happy. Yet, it will be well with those who fear God, no matter if their days are many or few.[102]

Spiritual happiness

Much is promised spiritually to those who fear the Lord. For this reason they are spoken of as the happiest of all people. The Lord is said to take pleasure in those who fear him and is noted as having the utmost complacency and delight in them being his special and peculiar people. His people are called his Hephzibah in whom he delights, and his Beulah to whom he is married.[103] They are made acceptable to him and therefore accepted by him. "Of a truth," says Peter, "I perceive that God is no respecter of persons, but in every

---

100 Psalm 34:7; Proverbs 14:26; 19:23.
101 Proverbs 10:27.
102 Ecclesiastes 8:12.
103 Psalm 147:11.

nation he that fears him and works righteousness, is accepted with him."[104] Those who fear him are made acceptable to him in Christ the beloved, and their sacrifices of prayer and praise are acceptable to God through Jesus Christ.

God's heart is near those who fear him. He has a sympathy and fellow feeling with them in all their distresses, trials, and exercises. God is afflicted in all their afflictions, and he comforts and supports them through those same afflictions. He is as a father who pities his children, so it is that the Lord pities those who fear him.[105]

The eye of the Lord is upon those who fear him for their own good, just as Scripture promises, "the eye of the Lord is upon them that fear him."[106] This speaks of his eye of providence which runs throughout the earth to show himself strong on their behalf, to protect and defend them, and to avenge himself on their enemies. Yet not only concerning providence, but also his eye of special love, grace, and mercy is upon those God-fearers and is never withdrawn from

---

104 Acts 10:34–35.
105 Psalm 103:13.
106 Psalm 33:18.

them. He ever delights in his people and so cares for them.[107] His hand is open and ready to communicate to them. He is ever mindful of his people and "gives meat to them that fear him,"[108] as in spiritual food which is the blessing of his covenant with them. The comforts of his Spirit sustain those who walk in the fear of the Lord. He gives them grace—fresh and rich supplies of it—and at last gives them glory. Prior to this display of glory, he withholds no good thing from them to support their faith, encourage their hope, or engage their trust in him and dependence on him.

The secrets of the Lord's heart and gracious designs are disclosed to those who fear him just as he said, "The secret of the Lord is with them that fear him."[109] He uses these disclosures so as to make his people his most intimate and dearest friends. He will show them his covenant, the blessings and promises of it, and why it must be of interest to them. He will show what is said of Christ the head of the covenant and what is true of all those marked in his

---

107 Psalm 103:11, 17; Luke 1:50.
108 Psalm 111:5.
109 Psalm 25:14.

covenant.[110] Added to this, the Lord grants the requests and fulfils the desires of those who fear him, he hears their cries, and he saves them.[111]

Those who fear God are remembered by him with the favour he bears to his own people. He remembers them with his tender mercies and lovingkindness which have been ever of old. He remembers them when they are in a low estate and brings them out of it. He remembers his promises to his people and fulfils them all. Scripture attests to God's memory of his beloved people, "a book of remembrance is" said to be "written before him, for those who feared the Lord."[112] It is promised to those "that fear the name" of the Lord that for their sake "the Son of righteousness will arise with healing in his wings."[113] Christ the Savior will come and show himself with a discovery and application of pardoning grace and mercy. Yes, to the one who fears the Lord, though he may walk in darkness—without any light—yet he is still encouraged to "trust in the name of the Lord, and rely on his

---

110 Malachi 2:5.
111 Psalm 145:19.
112 Malachi 3:16.
113 Malachi 4:2.

God."[114]

A renewed sense, interest, enjoyment, and recognizable application of salvation "is near to those who fear the Lord.[115] This sense of salvation is nearer to the believer than when they first believed. This fear of God is to grow ever nearer that when it was first planted by God, before they were stirred to seek after it, and had first hoped in it.

For those who fear God, great and good things are laid up in the heart of God, in the covenant of grace, in the hands of Christ, and in heaven. Such grand things include a blessed hope, a crown of righteousness, and all of which no eye has seen, ear heard, or anything conceived in the heart of man. "O how great is your goodness, which you have laid up for those who fear you!"[116]

---

[114] Isaiah 50:10.
[115] Psalm 85:9.
[116] Psalm 31:19.

FOUR

Wisdom

Zeal without wisdom is ignorant. Unless zeal is tempered with prudence it will be rash and hasty. I say wisdom or prudence because they are much the same thing, and go together, "I, wisdom, dwell with prudence."[1] Hence, wisdom and prudence, and the characters of wise and prudent, are often mentioned together. Prudence is wisely fixing on a right end of all actions, wisely choosing the best means conducive to that end, and using those means at the best time and in the most proper manner. As Scripture indicates, "the wisdom of the prudent is to understand his way"[2] in divine and spiritual things, to understand the way of salvation, the

---

1   Proverbs 8:12.
2   Proverbs 14:8.

way of his duty, and how to glorify God. Throughout this chapter, the term wisdom will include wisdom *and* prudence.

What is spiritual wisdom?

Spiritual wisdom is an internal grace, or inward disposition of the mind, respecting divine things. These divine things concern a man's duty, the salvation of his soul, and the glory of God.

A wisdom in the heart

In general, spiritual wisdom is a grace in the heart, so referred to as "wisdom in the hidden part."[3] The heart is often considered the true, hidden man. So it is that the wisdom of the heart is only demonstrated in hearty and sincere profession of religion. This profession of religion is shown through outward actions that are consistent with what is hidden in the heart, hence those who are truly wise, are said to be "wise in heart." As Scripture relates, "The wise in heart shall be called prudent,"[4] and so prudence fits a man,

3   Psalm 51:6.
4   Proverbs 16:21.

"when wisdom enters into his heart."[5] This wisdom is not original to the man and certainly not produced from out of the heart. Spiritual wisdom comes from elsewhere, from outside the man, from above, from God who puts it there in the heart of man and begins its blossom. The heart of man is naturally foolish; as much as the heart is desperately wicked, so it is equally foolish. Scripture says, "Their foolish heart was darkened,"[6] yet this is said of some thought to be very wise! Man is foolish by nature or more specifically from the moment of birth. Job records, "a stupid man will get understanding when a wild donkey's colt is born a man!"[7] As stupid as that creature is, so foolish is the heart of man apart from the Spirit. Foolishness is bound in the heart of every child of Adam, it is only the power of divine grace that can drive it far from him.

It is the case of every man that not one can understand divine and spiritual things,[8] or things pertaining to salvation. There are none who can know God, glorify him as

---

5   Proverbs 2:10.
6   Romans 1:21.
7   Job 11:12.
8   Romans 3:11.

God, or be thankful for mercies received from him. This is not only true of a few illiterate men or of such who have not the advantage of a good education, but even of the wisest philosophers that ever were in this world. Scripture speaks of these wise worldly men as those who, "professing themselves to be wise, they became fools."[9] Yes, this is the case, and this the character even of God's elect while unregenerate, until the grace of God takes place in their hearts: "We ourselves also were sometimes foolish."[10]

There is enough carnal wisdom in this world, there is enough wicked subtlety, of all that is earthly, sensual, and devilish. Worldly men are shrewder in the things of evil than they are to seek any knowledge of good,[11] but in respect of wisdom they are foolish, sottish, and without understanding.[12] They are quick and fruitful in inventing evil things, but cannot think a good thought. Men have no true spiritual wisdom but what God gives them or puts into them. God alone makes men to know wisdom in the

---

9 Romans 1:21–22.
10 Titus 3:3.
11 Luke 16:8.
12 Jeremiah 4:22.

heart experimentally; it is a gift of his "for the Lord gives wisdom."[13]

A right knowledge of self

Spiritual wisdom includes a right knowledge of man's self; "know thyself" was a maxim much talked of among the philosophers but attained by none of them. These philosophers are observably swelled with pride, vanity, and self-conceit. No man that is wise in his own eyes and prudent in his own sight knows himself, for one that was wiser than any of them says, there is "more hope of a fool" than of such.[14] Whoever in his own conceit is wise and good, holy and righteous in himself, does not really know himself. Whoever imagines that he has touched the righteousness of the law and is blameless,[15] truly does not know himself.

A man that rightly knows himself, and is possessed of true wisdom, has knowledge of the sinfulness of his nature. A man with spiritual wisdom will know his internal lust as sinful, his indwelling sin and the exceeding sinfulness of it,

---

13   Proverbs 2:6.
14   Proverbs 26:12; 29:20.
15   Philippians 3:6.

and of the plague of his own heart that will lead him not to trust in it for any goodness. He knows his own inability to perform that which is good and knows that without Christ and his grace he can do nothing, therefore he will not presume upon or attempt anything in his own strength. A wise man knows the imperfection of his own righteousness and will not depend upon it or plead by it as if it was justifying righteousness before God. The wise man knows his soul sickness, his spiritual maladies and diseases, and that they are incurable by his own or anyone's efforts, excepting the great physician Christ. To Christ alone he applies for healing! The wise man knows his own poverty, and therefore seeks for true riches in Christ; gold to make him rich, white raiment with which to be clothed, and Christ himself, the pearl of great price. The spiritually wise one is willing to part with all, with sinful and righteous self because he knows his own folly and is ready to acknowledge what a foolish and ignorant creature he is. Until a man has learned this lesson, he does not know himself.[16]

---

16   1 Corinthians 3:18.

A knowledge of the glory of God

True spiritual wisdom is no other than "the light of the knowledge of the glory of God in the face of Jesus Christ,"[17] which God commands to shine in the hearts of men. While men are destitute of grace or true spiritual wisdom, they are "without God,"[18] without knowledge of him or his nature and perfections. They conceive of him as just like themselves and imagine that he is pleased with what they are pleased with, and that he judges things just as they do. They are unacquainted with the purity and holiness of his nature—he cannot take pleasure in sin! They are ignorant of his righteousness and therefore go about seeking to establish their own. They are strangers to the grace and mercy of God, as it is channeled in Christ and conveyed through him. Therefore, they depend upon the absolute mercy of God, without any consideration of the propitiatory sacrifice of Christ—yet the true light of the saving knowledge of God is in Christ. In Christ our sovereign God has displayed his mercy and grace, and proclaimed his name in Christ.[19]

17 2 Corinthians 4:6.
18 Ephesians 2:12.
19 Exodus 34:6–7.

All the divine perfections shine most illustriously in Christ, as he is the brightness of his Father's glory and the express image of his person. His light is displayed in the great work of redemption and salvation worked by him. True spiritual wisdom rests in knowledge of this glory.

A fear of the Lord

True spiritual wisdom is no other than the fear of the Lord; both David and Solomon say that "the fear of the Lord is the beginning of wisdom."[20] There is no wisdom in a man before the fear of the Lord is put into him. Only then does a man begin to be wise, not before. Earlier than either David or Solomon, Job says, "The fear of the Lord, that is wisdom, and to turn away from evil is understanding."[21] This fear includes the whole worship of God, internal and external, flowing from a principle of grace. Fear of the Lord takes into account the whole duty of man, which it is his wisdom to practice internally and externally.

---

20 Psalm 111:10; Proverbs 9:10.
21 Job 28:28.

Wisdom to salvation

Spiritual wisdom means being wise to salvation and in things regarding salvation. The Scriptures are said to be able to make a man wise to salvation;[22] he is a wise man indeed who is thus made wise. The wise man is the one who sees himself lost and undone and inquires the way of salvation. He says as the jailor did, "What must I do to be saved?"[23] This wise man is made to recognize that the way of salvation is by Christ and that there is salvation in him alone. Once aware, he appeals to Christ as the disciples did: "Lord save me, I am perishing!"[24]

Those who are ready to perish come to Christ, count the cost, and commit themselves to him. The wise say, as the leper did: "Lord, if you will, you can make me clean," save me![25] These believers build their souls as well as their faith and hope of the salvation on Christ, the good, the sure, and only foundation. As he is a wise master builder who lays this foundation, these believers are wise to salvation who

---

22   2 Timothy 3:15.
23   Acts 16:30.
24   Matthew 8:25.
25   Matthew 8:2.

build upon this Rock—their house stands safe against every storm, and the gates of hell can never prevail. They give up themselves to Christ alone and are saved. They value him as their prize and love him above all others. They rejoice in him as God their Savior and give him the glory of their salvation!

The practicality of wisdom
When spiritual wisdom is gifted to a believer, there is a change which takes place, observed through the new creature. The wisdom from God bears witness of the heavenly promises of the gospel. Even so, it bears this witness in practical ways through the believer's regenerate life. The following are some of these discernible witnesses of spiritual wisdom.

About good business
Spiritual wisdom is evidenced in doing good things. Those who are wickedly wise are wise to do evil, but those who are spiritually wise are "wise for that which is good" and

"simple concerning evil."[26] The spiritually wise are capable of doing things both for their own good and for the good of others. They may do good for themselves: "He that is wise may be profitable to himself."[27] In this case he may profit, and even if it is not for God, yet he profits for his present good, peace, and tranquility of mind. So, though the wisdom is not "for" God, yet it proves that "in" keeping the commands of God there is great reward and great peace of mind. Those who love and observe the law of God find this peace, even as they do not trust in and depend on observing the commands for their salvation to eternal life.

A wise believer may be useful to others. Believers in God are exhorted to maintain good works because they are "good and profitable to men."[28] This profitableness is demonstrated by their example and a real benefit to them. See that a wise man shows his wisdom through what he does and whatever he does may well honour his true religion. It may stop the mouths of gainsayers, it may shame those who speak ill of religion, and convict those false professors

---

26 Romans 16:19.
27 Job 22:2; Proverbs 9:12.
28 Titus 3:8.

of religion. The spiritually wise adorn the doctrine of God our Saviour and recommend it to others. By their good works and their conversations as shining evidence before men, they glorify God and win souls to him. Their spiritual wisdom is witnessed as they do right for all the right reasons and for the right end, for by spiritual wisdom they do all they do from love of God, for the faith and strength of Christ, and with a view to the glory of God. These believers are observed through the "meekness of wisdom,"[29] without trusting or boasting in themselves. They know that when they have done all they can they are but unprofitable servants. Truly, it is by the grace of God they are what they are, and do what they do.

Professing religious truth

This spiritual wisdom shows itself particularly in professing religious truth. The kingdom of heaven, or the visible church, is compared to ten virgins, "Five of them wise, and five foolish."[30] The foolish virgins, or foolish professors of religion, took the lamp of an outward profession, as the

29 James 3:13.
30 Matthew 25:2.

rest did, and were careful to trim it and keep it bright and shining. Yet, these foolish professors were not concerned for the oil of grace that would keep the lamp burning. The wise virgins not only took the lamp of profession, but they were concerned to have the oil of grace in the vessels of their hearts with their lamps and so continued burning until the bridegroom arrived. The wise professors showed their wisdom.

The spiritually wise hold fast their profession without wavering. Such are wise professors who steadfastly continue in their profession by keeping to the principles of grace, valuing mature consideration of the cost and charges, remain stalwart in difficulties and discouragements, and stay bold in the trials and tribulations they expect to meet. These wise believers have put their hand to the plough and neither turn or look back, but press on believing to the saving of their souls. Even so, they do not depend upon their profession, lean on it for refuge, or believe on their plea as if it were eternal life in itself. Some at the last day will plead that they have professed the name of Christ, embraced his gospel, and subjected themselves to his ordinances, but

Christ will say, "Depart from me; I never knew you!"[31]

Wise counseling and demeanor
Spiritual wisdom shows itself in a pleasant walk and demeanor. A spiritually wise demeanor is one that is ordered aright, according to the rule of the word of God, and ornamental to the gospel of Christ. This demeanor appears when a vigilant man walks with his eyes about him, perceiving where he is going, and discerning his steps as the prudent man does. His eyes look straight ahead pondering the path of his feet, neither turning to the right hand or to the left. This wise man walks in wisdom towards those who are without Christ as well as in peace and love towards those who are within Christ. He is careful to give no offence to Jew or Gentile or to the church of God. This wisdom is seen when professors walk not as fools, in a vain, careless, and sinful manner, but as wise. This wise walk is observed in believers when they walk as the word of God directs them, when they walk uprightly according to the gospel, when they walk as they have Christ for an example,

---

31   Matthew 7:22–23; Luke 13:25–26.

and when they walk not after the flesh but after the Spirit. One particularly special instance of walking wisely is, "redeeming the time, because the days are evil."[32] This is performed when they lose no opportunity of doing good to others or of receiving good for themselves. The wise consider their own days as evil and subject to many temptations, and that the days of old age are hasting on—when they will be incapable of doing or receiving good—they walk wisely and so redeem the time.[33]

Discerning of providence

This wisdom shows itself in observing the providence of God in the world, and its various eras. Wisdom is shown by making useful remarks upon how God used various means throughout history. Spiritual wisdom brings a man to learn useful lessons from providence. Scripture says, "Whoever is wise will observe these things," that is, things in providence, so that "they will understand the lovingkindness of the Lord."[34] Spiritual wisdom is shown to understand both

---

32   Ephesians 5:16.
33   Ephesians 5:15–16.
34   Psalm 107:43.

the ways of God in his providence, the ways and methods of God in his grace, and the ways he has prescribed his people to walk in.[35]

Heavenly prospect

This spiritual wisdom is revealed in a man's concern about his last end and future state. He desires to know how it will be with him at last, and how it will go with him in another world. He is concerned with how near it is and what that may come of it. He is ready for death to come whenever it will because he is eager for an eternal world![36]

On receiving spiritual wisdom

How we receive spiritual wisdom is a question put by Job, "From where, then, does wisdom come? And where is the place of understanding?" The answer comes to Job, "God understands the way to it, and he knows its place."[37] Spiritual wisdom comes from God. It is original to him and in full perfection. Yes, wisdom is in him as it is infinite and

---

35 Hosea 14:9.
36 Deuteronomy 32:29.
37 Job 28:20, 23.

unsearchable. It is his gift to bestow, and so it is to be asked only of him who gives to all men liberally, freely, richly, and bountifully, as any has need. God's wisdom is given graciously even to those in whom there is fault because of former foolishness, ingratitude, and lack of improvement from what they had received.[38]

Wisdom comes from God alone

God is the efficient cause of wisdom; that is, God the Father, the Son, and the Spirit. Wisdom is a good and perfect gift from above, and comes from the Father of lights, the King eternal, immortal, invisible, the only wise God, the fountain of all wisdom. God makes men in common wiser than the fowls of the heaven, and his saints wiser in spiritual things than the rest of mankind. Spiritual wisdom comes from Christ who is the only wise God and our Saviour. Christ is the wisdom of God, whose is counsel and sound wisdom, and who is made to us wisdom. The Spirit of wisdom rests on Christ, and in him are all the treasures of wisdom and knowledge. This spiritual wisdom only comes by

---

38   James 1:5.

the Spirit of wisdom and revelation in the knowledge of Christ.

The word of God is the means for obtaining wisdom
The means of promoting and increasing God's wisdom are the word of God, the ministers of his word, and good men well versed in it. The Scriptures read and explained, when under a divine influence and accompanied with divine power, are "able to make wise for salvation."[39] The Scriptures are written for our learning, for the ministers of God's gospel who show men the way of salvation, and those who "win" souls to Christ—those who are "wise" and make wise. This means of learning the word, and conversation with wise and good men concerning it, is a means of increasing wisdom, as it reads, "walk with the wise and become wise."[40]

Wisdom according to James 3:17

A full account of the nature and properties of spiritual wisdom is evidenced through James 3:17.

---

39 2 Timothy 3:15.
40 Proverbs 11:30; 13:20.

Wisdom is "from above," from God; Father, Son, and Spirit. As before observed, spiritual wisdom is conversant about heavenly things. It is celestial wisdom that stands opposed to earthly wisdom as in a preceding verse—wisdom about earthly things, the wisdom of this world, and the princes of it that all come to nothing.

Wisdom is "pure" in itself and in its effects. It produces purity of heart, life, and conversation. The effect of wisdom is pure and undefiled observances of religion. Those who have wisdom hold the mystery of the faith in a pure conscience and they are obedient to the divine precepts as out of a pure heart and a faith unfeigned. Spiritual wisdom is opposed to that wisdom that is sensual, employed in sensual gratifications, and to carnal wisdom, as Scripture calls it the "wisdom of the flesh,"[41] or carnal mind, which bears enmity against God.

Wisdom is "peaceable." It influences those who profess it to be at peace among themselves, and with one another. The wise will live peaceably, as much as possible, with all men. They will cultivate peace in families, among

---

41 Romans 8:7.

neighbors, and even with enemies.

Wisdom is said to be "gentle." It makes those who have it to be gentle towards all men, moderate, and humane. Wisdom brings men to bear and forbear; that is, to bear the infirmities of the weak and to forbear and forgive one another for any injury. The wise will forfeit their own just rights for the sake of peace and love. They will not deal harshly with others for their failings but cover them with the mantle of love.

Wisdom is "easy to be entreated," or persuaded. The wise will put up with affronts and will gladly condescend to men of low estate, and not mind high things. The wise know that "with the lowly is wisdom." They yield easily to the superior judgment and stronger reasonings of others and are readily inclined and induced to hope and believe the best of all men. They entertain a good opinion of good men and their conduct.

Wisdom is "full of mercy and good fruits." It fills men with compassion on those in distress. It leads men to act with benevolence to the poor according to their ability; that is, to feed and clothe them, to visit widows and orphans in their affliction and so comfort them. It leads men to do other duties and good works as fruits of righteousness of the grace of God, and of the Spirit.

Wisdom is "without partiality." Wisdom is not partial to the wise themselves, or in esteeming each other better than themselves. A wise man will not show favoritism with respect of persons because he sees no difference between rich and poor in Christian fellowship. He will give to the poor and needy without distinction, favor, or affectation.

Wisdom is "without hypocrisy." A wise man will not make a show of what they do not have or do not intend to do—whether to God or man. As wisdom is a grace, it has a close connection with faith unfeigned, with hope which is without hypocrisy, and with love which is without dissimulation.

All of this exegesis shows how useful and desirable spiritual wisdom is. It is necessary throughout the conduct of a Christian life. Only with spiritual wisdom can a Christian do his duty, avoid the snares and temptations to which he is liable, to seek his own good, pursue the good of others, and above all seek the glory of God.

Discussion Questions

Chapter One: Fortitude

1. How would you describe the difference between worldly courage and spiritual fortitude?
2. Why is a Christian called to exercise fortitude? How has this characteristic challenged you in the past? How does fortitude through suffering and affliction serve to raise affection for Christ?
3. How have you previously failed to exercise fortitude? In hindsight, how would a right understanding of Christian fortitude have served you in sanctification through your trials?
4. Why does Gill include death as a key argument for Christian fortitude? How do you agree/disagree with this example?
5. What is the relationship between human responsibility

in fortitude and the gifting of fortitude in the graces of the Spirit?

Chapter 2: Zeal

1. Looking at the picture Gill gives of zeal, how would you differentiate a human passion from a Christian zeal?
2. Where in your life have you considered your zeal may have been a false emotionalism (mistaken, superstitious, ignorant, etc.)? Why might doctrine and zeal serve one another in combating this?
3. What are some ways Christians can make other things the object of zeal? How can we guard our churches for true zeal?
4. Gill argues that "the love of Christ in redeeming his people will constrain them…in doctrine and practice," how does this constraining work? What is the responsibility on the part of God's people?
5. How does duty in religious practice shepherd an otherwise wayward zeal?

Chapter 3: The Fear of God

1. To believers and unbelievers alike, why is the phrase

"fear of God" frequently received with negative connotations?
2. What is it about God that should bring reverence and awe to his worshippers?
3. How does Gill describe the fear of or worship of each person in the Triune God? Why is this useful for the church to consider?
4. Given the examples of the various kinds of fear, how have you encountered different kinds of misguided fears? How would you help to correct them now?
5. How does fear of God, an awe and reverence, lead to obedience without devolving into slavish or idolatrous fear?

Chapter 4: Wisdom
1. Why is wisdom "in the heart" such an important phrase? How does this connect to Gill's argument that wisdom is a gift from God?
2. How does spiritual wisdom relate to fortitude, zeal, and fear of God?
3. What is the connection between spiritual wisdom and being made "wise unto salvation"?

DISCUSSION QUESTIONS

4. How are Christians to use spiritual wisdom even though we may be surrounded by worldly neighbors? What does this example look like?
5. What are your impressions from Gill's exegesis of James 3:17? How does this strengthen the discussion for spiritual wisdom?

Scripture Index

OLD TESTAMENT

Genesis
3:9	16
3:10	100
20:11	113
22:12	113
31:42	89
31:53	89

Exodus
34:6-7	131

Leviticus
19:3	86
19:14	111

Deuteronomy
4:10	115
5:29	114
6:13	89
6:25	62
10:12	89
10:20	89
17:19	115
28:58	90
32:39	140
33:25	42

Joshua
1:9	46
24:15	38

1 Samuel
12:18	87

2 Samuel
10:12	47

1 Kings
18:21	72

2 Kings
10:16	68
29-31	68

2 Chronicles
19:7	94

Nehemiah
5:15	110

Job
1:1	104, 109
1:9	98
4:6	99
11:12	127

SCRIPTURE INDEX

13:15	104
15:4	98
19:25	104
22:2	135
28:20	140
28:23	140
28:28	109, 115, 132
37:22-23	93-94

Psalms

2:11	86, 104
5:7	86
7:2	37
19:7, 9	116
25:14	121
27:1	43, 105
27:3-4	43, 105
27:14	56
31:19	104, 123
33:8	94
33:18	120
34:7	119
34:9-10	117
34:11	115
35:17	37
36:1	114
37:16	118
45:11	86
51:6	115, 126
53:5	97
57:4	37
69:9	77, 81
73:25	71, 104
85:9	123
86:11	116
89:7	86
97:10	106
103:11	121
103:13	120
107:43	139
111:5	121
111:10	115, 132
112:1, 3	118
112:9	90
115:11	104
119:113	107
119:120	96
119:128	108
128:1-4	118
130:4	95, 116
139:21-22	108
145:19	122
147:11	119

Proverbs

2:3-5	116
2:6	129
2:10	127
3:7	109
4:14-15	108, 110
8:12	125
8:13	106, 108
9:10	115, 132
9:12	135
10:27	119
11:30	142
13:20	142
14:8	125
14:16	109
14:26	119
15:16	117
16:6	109
16:18	118
16:21	126
18:14	44
19:23	119
22:4	118
24:10	44

24:21	87	***Micah***	
26:12	129	4:2	91
28:1	37	4:5	83
29:20	129		
30:30	34	***Haggai***	
		2:4	41

Ecclesiastes
5:7	107
7:26	50
8:12	119
12:13	85

Zechariah
1:14	60
8:2	60

Malachi
1:6	87
2:5	122
3:16	122
4:2	122

Song of Solomon
3:7	47
8:6-7	59

Isaiah
2:19, 21	96
8:13	91
8:13-14	92
9:7	60
11:12	55
33:6	118
41:10	42
41:17-18	117
43:19-20	117
50:10	123
53	17
63:10	92

NEW TESTAMENT

Matthew
28:20	41

Mark
6:20	87

Luke
1:50	121
1:74-75	99
9:55	66
13:25-26	138
16:18	128
20:13	92

Jeremiah
5:22	94
5:24	95
10:7	87
10:10	97
32:39-40	114

John
2:17	81
8:3, 9	69
12:5-6	69

Hosea
3:5	91, 95, 116

SCRIPTURE INDEX

Acts
5:29	42
10:34-35	120
13:50	68
16:30	133
17:22	67, 97
18:25	79
21:20	66
22:3	68

Romans
1:17	63
2:2	61
3:20	64
3:21-22	63
3:24	64
3:26	61
3:28	64
4:6	64
5:9	64
7:15	108
8:35, 38-39	57
9:32	63
13:7	86

1 Corinthians
2:2	17
3:18	130
12:31	80
14:1	80
14:12	80
14:19	80
15:55	51
16:13	34

2 Corinthians
2:17	74
4:6	131
6:16, 18	96
7:1	96
7:7	80
9:2	75
11:2	60

Galatians
1:14	66
3:10	101
4:1	37
4:15	70
4:18	82
6:17	45

Ephesians
2:12	131
3:14	54
3:16	54-55
5:15-16	139
5:33	86
6:1-2	86
6:5	86

Philippians
1:28	48
2:12-13	105
3:3	105
3:6	68, 129
3:8	71
3:9	63

Colossians
1:11-12	54
4:12	80

2 Timothy
1:7	33
2:1	38
3:15	133, 142

SCRIPTURE INDEX

Titus
2:14	80, 82
3:3	128, 135

Hebrews
9:27	52
10:34	45
11:36	45
12:1-3	57
12:9, 28	86

James
1:5	141
3:13	136
3:17	142, 150
5:16	80

1 Peter
1:14	86
1:17	86
1:22	80
2:7-8	92
3:5-6	86
4:8	80

1 John
2:14	55
4:4-5	49
4:18	57, 103

Jude
1:3	48

Revelation
2:2	77
3:15-16	72, 82
3:19-20	82
12:11	55
14:13	51
21:8	89

THE *John Gill* **PROJECT**

The eminent Baptist pastor-theologian John Gill (1697–1771) is a towering figure in Baptist thought and life. The late D. Martyn Lloyd-Jones thought of Gill as "a man, not only of great importance in his own century, but a man who is still of great importance to all of us." But more than a mere Baptist theologian, the growing retrieval movement of classically Reformed orthodox theology also places Gill among the greatest theologians in the Great Tradition. Therefore, The London Lyceum, The Andrew Fuller Center, and H&E Publishing have partnered together to form the John Gill Project with the mission to republicize the work of John Gill for a new generation of pastors, students, and scholars in dire need of historical resources that remain resolutely committed to classic orthodox Christian doctrine.

www.ingramcontent.com/pod-product-compliance
Lightning Source LLC
Chambersburg PA
CBHW021108080526
44587CB00010B/441